Rickwood

PRAISE FOR "RICKWOOD: HOW AMERICA'S OLDEST BALLPARK FORGED BASEBALL'S LEGENDS"

"During my time working in baseball, I've felt part of my job is to help a ballpark tell its own story. Each one is so distinctive and such a reflection of its city and place in the cultural lore of the land. Now comes Tim Whitt and Joe Mock to serve as the voice for Rickwood Field. And what stories Rickwood Field can tell after over 100 years, from its legacy as the sibling of the storied Shibe Park/Connie Mack Stadium in Philadelphia to the moment when the national spotlight coincided with the passing of Birmingham's own Willie Mays. This book is about more than baseball; it's a reflection of the last hundred years of our nation's cultural history, Birmingham's place in that story, and a reminder of why baseball is America's Pastime."

—**Janet Marie Smith**, co-founder of Canopy Team and and planning executive for Camden Yards, Dodger Stadium, Fenway Park, and Turner Field

"Rickwood will educate all of us and further explain how our baseball hearts and souls fall in love with these beautiful parks where we spend hours and hours of our lives and dream our own personal baseball dreams."

—**Mike Capps,** baseball broadcaster and author of *Grinders: Baseball's Intrepid Infantry* and *The Scout: Searching for the Best in Baseball*

"My grandfather would have loved this book, because it does a beautiful job of describing the history of the ballpark he built and loved."

—**Rick Woodward III**, grandson of the builder of Rickwood Field

"Joe Mock and Tim Whitt capture the complete story of Rickwood Field. Our City is honored to maintain such a special place. There is a great deal of community pride in offering this landmark to our residents as well as baseball fans from around the world."

—**Randall L. Woodfin**, Mayor of the City of Birmingham

"Rickwood is a place of pilgrimage, a sacred space where the past whispers stories of struggle and perseverance to the present. Leveraging deep research, driven by infectious curiosity, Tim Whitt and Joe Mock show readers why and how the complicated past of this fabled stadium can inspire our collective future."

—**John T. Edge,** writer and host of the Emmy-winning television show *TrueSouth* on ESPN

"Rickwood Field is steeped in history and stands tall through the rigors of time and American progress. Tim Whitt and Joe Mock paint a vivid picture of the history of this classic American treasure as well as the barnstorming legends and Negro Leagues immortals who have come through its gates. In my book, Mock is the authority on ballparks. He observes and writes about them with a care and precision that brings them to life. We have trusted him as our ballpark expert for more than a decade."

—**Stephen Borelli,** editor, *USA TODAY Sports Weekly* and author of *How About That! The Life of Mel Allen*

"Who could have predicted that a ballpark built in a Southern industrial city during the Taft administration would be still with us today? The history of Rickwood Field is a microcosm of the history of America, and this book synthesizes its myriad eras and improbable twists and turns into a compelling page-turner. Here's to another 100+ years of baseball in Birmingham's Minor League – and now Major League – cathedral."

—**Benjamin Hill**, author of The Baseball Traveler Newsletter that covers Minor League Baseball for MLB

"When you write about something you love, as Joe and Tim have done with RICKWOOD, it's not work. It's pleasure. Reading this, I felt like I was on a magic carpet ride, looking down on over 100 years of baseball royalty. And I especially enjoyed the deep dive on Rick Woodward. If there's a Mount Rushmore of Birminghamians, he'd be on it."

—**Curt Bloom**, for 33 years the play-by-play voice of the Birmingham Barons

"I've spent the majority of the last 42 years in ballparks, but never have I seen a history of a park as complete and as touching as RICKWOOD. This is a must-read for anyone with the slightest interest in baseball history."

—**Jay Miller**, former executive for the Texas Rangers and the Minor League teams in Eugene, Salem, Port Charlotte, New Orleans, Round Rock, Sugar Land and Wichita

"For years, I've covered the business of baseball, particularly as it relates to ballparks. I've long considered Joe Mock's authentic, rigorous, and entertaining reviews of stadiums the gold standard. That comes through on every page of RICKWOOD, as he and Tim Whitt provide us with an immersive, stimulating portrait of one of the sport's most legendary shrines. Their telling of the birth of the Negro Leagues and the 1931 Dixie Series by themselves are worth the price of the book."

—**Alan Poff**, webmaster of Ballparkbiz.com

Rickwood

HOW AMERICA'S OLDEST BALLPARK FORGED BASEBALL'S LEGENDS

TIM WHITT & JOE MOCK

Stoney Creek Publishing

Stoney Creek Publishing®

Rickwood: How America's Oldest Ballpark Forged Baseball's Legends

ISBN: 978-1-965766-52-1

ISBN (Hardcover): 978-1-965766-54-5

ISBN (Ebook): 978-1-965766-53-8

Library of Congress Control Number: 2025926579

Cover and Interior design by Kimberly James

Cover photos by Joe Mock and Friends of Rickwood Field

All photographs on pages 19, 28-29, 38,46-47, 56, 60, 70, 72-73, 76, 84, 86, 88, 92, 95, 97-99, 103-105, 122 provided by Friends of Rickwood. Used with permission.

All photos on pages 101-102, 121, 137-139, 143-145, 151, 155, 157, 159, 161-162, 167 by Joe Mock.

Photo on page 140 by Graham Knight. Used with permission.

This book is not endorsed by Major League Baseball or any of its clubs.

Printed in U.S.A.

"I think now that there had to be many fathers who left work, then came home on Sept. 16, 1931 in Birmingham with hats pushed back, with songs in the voices that lighted the eyes of their sons because Ray Caldwell had won, and this surely was the happiest day anyone had ever known anywhere. That's the way it was with baseball then."

—Benny Marshall, the late spots editor of the *Birmingham News,* on the legendary opening game of the Dixie Series of 1931.

CONTENTS

Foreword by Joe Mock	13
Introduction: Fathers and Sons by Tim Whitt	17
1. A New Game for the New South	23
2. The Name Above the Gate	27
3. "As Near Perfect as Skill and Money Could Make It"	32
4. "Beneath a Halo of Incomparable Glory"	41
5. Young Stubblebeard	45
6. A Putting Away of Childish Things	50
7. "The Fastest and Hardest Ball in the Circuit"	55
8. The Babe of the Bush	65
9. Summer and Smoke	69
10. Dizzy and Ray	75
11. The Chill Rains Come	83
12. Nighttime Baseball	86
13. The Glennon Years	90
14. A Real American Holy Place	96
15. A Schoolboy from Fairfield	101

16. Years Without Summers 107

17. Rumpled, Childish Souls Who Go to Games for Free: Rickwood's Rooftop Legends 113

18. Charlie O. and Reggie 119

19. Indian Summer 125

20. A Tree Grows in Atlanta: How the Movies and a Cracker Saved Rickwood Field 130

21. Ending a Decade of Friction 137

22. Swearing on My Mother's Grave 146

23. Ensuring the Legacy 150

24. Sea Lions and Stars 154

25. Fathers and Sons ... and Grandsons 164

INDEX 169

ABOUT THE AUTHORS 179

FOREWORD

BY JOE MOCK

I want to tell you about a romance. It's a romance that started a quarter-century ago and has blossomed into this book.

As the nation was untangling from the "Y2K" conundrum at the beginning of 2000, I moved from Maryland to Texas. The moving van was coming later, so I made the 1,500-mile drive myself. As a lifelong ballpark fan who started BaseballParks.com at the dawn of the newfangled World Wide Web in 1997, I knew I wanted to map a route to visit some ballparks along the way.

One in particular.

I'd heard about Birmingham's Rickwood Field for years, and now I had the opportunity to see it for myself. I didn't want to show up to a padlocked facility, so I contacted the group known as Friends of Rickwood to say I wanted to visit. The executive director of FOR at the time was David Brewer, and he graciously met me at the park on a bitterly cold, rain-soaked day.

I was an excited visitor as he showed me all aspects of the ninety-year-old facility. I couldn't get over how beautiful it was. And I'd never seen a treasure also have such a sense of history about it. No doubt about it, I was falling in love.

At the small merchandise table at Rickwood, I spotted a book that seemed to call out to me. It was called *Bases Loaded With History*. Timothy Whitt had authored the book five years earlier.

I was happy to support the Friends of Rickwood by purchasing the book, and I packed it away and continued on my drive to Texas, intending to add this book to my already-too-large library of ballpark-related publications.

But once I started to read *Bases Loaded With History*, I couldn't put it down. Whitt's beautiful descriptions of the Negro League teams and the historic 1931 Dixie Series really spoke to me. He was a master storyteller, and page by page I was falling more in love with the ballpark at the heart of his vignettes and anecdotes.

On my website, I'm known for ranking everything—the ballparks with the best views, the best concessions, etc. Well, *Bases Loaded With History* zoomed up my ranking of favorite books, tying in the top spot with the marvelous *Lost Ballparks* by the brilliant, late Lawrence Ritter. The two tomes were similar in that they lovingly told the stories of baseball stadiums built long ago. It was downright depressing how many of those edifices had been demolished in decades past, cast aside in the name of progress. But not Rickwood, which still stood proudly in Birmingham's West End.

And the fact that it is still around is a blessing of the highest order.

Reading Whitt's book once wasn't nearly enough. So I reread it, highlighted favorite passages, and made notes in the margins. I kept reaching for it again and again, like a puppy that never stops looking adoringly at its human owner.

I knew I wanted to see Rickwood again, this time in all its splendor with two ball clubs duking it out. When I read that the venerable park was going to host the Rickwood Classic in 2010 as part of the celebration of its 100th birthday, I knew I had to go. So I played hooky from work that day, catching a flight to Birmingham early in the morning and flying back home that night—in much the same way that businessmen in the Magic City had snuck away from their desks to attend the park's grand opening on August 18, 1910, or to experience the biggest faceoff in Rickwood's history when Dizzy "Tain't braggin' if you kin really do it" Dean took the mound against aging Ray Caldwell in the Dixie Series on September 16, 1931.

And I knew all about these milestones because of Whitt's book.

I got away with it, as my bosses never learned I'd snuck off to Birmingham that afternoon. And everything about that day was simply glorious.

When I would come back to town to review the Barons' new Regions Field home, or to present its owners with a plaque for BaseballParks.com's Ballpark of the Year, I made a point to pay my respects to the grand old lady in the West End. After all, she'd captured my heart years before and had never let go.

It was a thrill to represent *USA TODAY* at a three-day event that Major League Baseball staged at Rickwood in June of 2024. I wrote preview after preview for the publication, and while at the MLB game, filed reports for USATODAY.com. You can still see a lot of my reporting on it at BaseballParks.com.

And whom did I chase down for quotes for those preview articles? The man I was delighted to learn was still walking the rich, red clay of Alabama: Tim Whitt. I asked him if we could get together for barbecue and a game in his hometown of Montgomery while I was in the area. And, of course, I begged him to autograph *Bases Loaded With History* for me. It was a fairly ragged, dog-eared copy after twenty-four years of my reading and rereading it, but I was very happy to get his signature on it.

During that meeting, we hatched the possibility of writing an updated version of his book. After all, even with no daily tenant at Rickwood, much had happened in the three decades since he first wrote his book. So much more was now known about the Negro Leagues. And I had mounds of great materials and interviews from the three days that MLB had spent in the Magic City in 2024. Plus, the big-league execs had made commitments to host more events in the future.

Slowly but surely, a plan came together for Tim and I to write a greatly expanded version of his 1995 book, and we're grateful that you are now holding it in your hands. It contains at least 12,000 more words than the original and features not only lots of details you won't find anywhere else about the last thirty years of Rickwood history, but also tremendous new insights and perspectives into the early years of the Barons and Black Barons. I don't know how Tim was able to gather so much information for the original book, since it predated the era of ubiquitous internet resources that we now take for granted. But now we are able to research and unearth so many more stories about the unparalleled and colorful characters who are brought to life in these pages.

And without a doubt, Rickwood's stately grandstands have seen more history than any other ballpark used by the Negro Leagues or the minor leagues.

So I couldn't be more excited for you to read about the object of my affections: America's Oldest Ballpark.

Joe Mock
Webmaster of BaseballParks.com
Sports facilities writer for *USA TODAY*

INTRODUCTION

FATHERS AND SONS

BY TIM WHITT

"Baseball is fathers and sons," wrote noted writer Donald Hall, a Poet Laureate of the United States, in his essay *Fathers Playing Catch With Sons.* "Football is brothers beating each other up in the backyard, violent and superficial. Baseball is the generations, looping backward forever with a million apparitions of sticks and balls, cricket and rounders, and the games the Iroquois played in Connecticut before the English came. Baseball is fathers and sons playing catch, lazy and murderous, wild and controlled, the profound archaic song of birth, growth, age, and death. The diamond encloses what we are."

A man I never met introduced me to Rickwood Field. If the reader will allow me a few moments to tell a true story, I believe I can explain how a ghost led me to a ballpark of phantoms.

William Putnam lived in Birmingham until he passed away in 1973. A heart attack claimed him while still a young man, at the age of forty-one. Many years after his death, a relative visited his widow one afternoon. Alongside an old-style stereo cabinet that sat unused and unnoticed in a corner of the living room was an LP record album.

The album was titled *Stan the Man's Big Hit Record.* Intrigued, the visitor played the scratchy old record and discovered that (thankfully) Stan Musial had not taken up crooning as a sideline as his career declined in the early 1960s. Instead, the record was instructional in nature, as the St. Louis Cardinals' greatest player talked about how he developed the skills that enabled him to attain the then-astronomical total of 3,000 hits.

Stan the Man discussed the proper batting stance with Joe Garagiola. As he listened, it dawned on the visitor why Mr. Putnam bought this record. It was actually for his son. The fondest dream of William, a lifelong Cardinals fan, was for the boy to learn to hit a baseball like the Great Musial did.

All of this was news to the visitor. By this time, William had become an image in a family portrait, the painted color of the photograph fading along with his memory. The very color and nature of the man were fading with time as well. His character, who he *was*, were things his grandson, born nineteen years after William's death, would one day want to know about his grandfather.

The Musial record album became a Rosetta Stone of the life of William Putnam. Suddenly there were things that could be discovered about this man—his tastes, his inclinations, his priorities. And he was a devoted Cardinals fan! The Cards had long been the team of choice in the Deep South, since the Washington Senators and the Cincinnati Reds had never met with much success. And in William's time, the Atlanta Braves were newcomers to the region, still "too new" to capture the hearts of longtime fans.

William Putnam's friends and relatives confirmed that he followed the fortunes of the Cardinals. But they were always quick to point out that he lived and died with the Birmingham Barons, the local minor league team that inhabited Rickwood Field, already considered a "venerable" park in the middle years of the 20th century. On summer days in the late 1940s, a teenaged William Putnam often caught the streetcar that ran in front of his home on 1st Avenue North in Birmingham's East Lake neighborhood, bound for the West End and the bleachers of Rickwood. There, he braved the oppressive heat to cheer for Walt Dropo and George Wilson and all the other Barons idols of the golden postwar era of Birmingham baseball.

It was a wonderful time to be a baseball fan in Birmingham.

The great players of the major leagues played at Rickwood in those days, too. Every year, as they made their way north to start the season after spring training in Florida, the big-league clubs stopped in Birmingham to play exhibitions. Young William sat in the bleachers at Rickwood as a parade of Hall of Famers passed before him on the diamond: Joe DiMaggio ... Ted Williams ... Warren Spahn ...

And Stan Musial.

It was Stan the Man who seized the imagination of young William. Years later, when he had a boy of his own, William wanted his son to be like the Cardinals outfielder. At Rickwood Field, a teenage boy had found a hero he took into manhood with him, to hand down to that son.

MIGHTY ROAR—Stan Musial gets a handshake from Red Schoendienst after he hit a tremendous homer over the scoreboard on the roof of the right field stands. This took place in the fourth inning yesterday. Standing on the left waiting to bat is Ray Jablonski. The White Sox catcher is Red Wilson. The Cards beat the White Sox, 7-4. (Staff Photos by Jim Robbins.)

Stan Musial greeted at home by Red Schoendienst after hitting titanic homer in Rickwood, April 1, 1954

Putnam's devotion to The Man is touching. My own father loved Ted Williams. I can still hear him cussing Curt Gowdy ("Talks too much!") on the NBC Game of the Week while disparaging modern-day players with endless comparisons to the Splendid Splinter. "What is that guy hitting? And he gets HOW MUCH money? Ted Williams could beat that RIGHT NOW. Best hitter ever. Woulda broke all the records if he hadn't gone off in the service. He was the best, the best ever."

I believe that William Putnam and my father were not that different. They had both chosen heroes in their adolescence from the baseball stars of the era, and they had followed their idols through the years, from their brilliant youths in the early 1940s to their twilight in the early 1960s. My father (I have always believed) admired Ted Williams because they had both served in the United States Marine Corps in the Korean War. Why had William Putnam chosen Stan Musial as his hero?

It's only a hunch, but it is a hunch that I feel in my soul. Young William was probably in Rickwood Field the day that Stan Musial hit a titanic home run "over the Negro bleachers," as the sportswriters of the time reported. William would never have forgotten the force of Stan the Man's bat, the sound of the ball striking Stan's

Louisville Slugger, the arc of the ball as it escaped the confines of Rickwood Field. William Putnam found something heroic in Stan Musial that day in Rickwood, something that he wanted to give to his son. And to his grandson.

And he did give that gift. Because that grandson is my son.

As Doris Kearns Goodwin wrote in *From Father With Love*, "There is magic in the moment, for when I open my eyes and see my sons in the place where my father once sat, I feel an invisible bond between our three generations, an anchor of loyalty linking my sons to the grandfather whose face they never saw but whose person they have already come to know through this most timeless of all sports, baseball."

The Game, and the ballpark, joins us. Generation to generation, across the years, and across the barriers in men's minds.

Born in the same year as William Putnam, but on the other side of Birmingham—as well as on the other side of an immense, invisible divide of another kind—was Willie Howard Mays Jr. Young Willie, like young William, went to Rickwood Field at every opportunity. His father, who worked in the steel mills of Fairfield, took Willie to the games. When the Birmingham Barons played, Willie and his father sat in the "Negro bleachers," exposed to the hot sun in distant right field. But when the Birmingham Black Barons of the Negro American League played at Rickwood Field, Willie could sit in the grandstand, in seats that were normally reserved for whites. From the "good" seats, Willie and his father could watch Josh Gibson, "Cool Papa" Bell, and Satchel Paige, although Willie's hero was the New York Yankees' center fielder, Joe DiMaggio. It was a wonderful time to be a fan of Black baseball in Birmingham, although it was not a wonderful time to be *Black* in Birmingham.

Willie's father was a ballplayer, and a good one. Even as Willie Jr. reached adulthood, Willie Sr. was still a star of the industrial leagues. The elder Mays always had time to work with his son, developing his fledgling skills, even when the father was exhausted from a long day in the mills.

As a teenager, Willie joined his father in the industrial leagues.

One day a ball was hit between the two Mayses in the outfield. Young Willie called his father off the ball, knowing that the old man could not reach it. Willie Jr. made the catch; Willie Sr. never played again.

Not long after hanging up his own glove, Willie Mays Sr. took his son to meet Piper Davis, the playing manager of the Birmingham Black Barons. The father and the manager talked while the son waited. Then Willie Mays Sr. left the ballpark, leaving his son to live out his own dreams of roaming the outfield of Rickwood Field, while the old man went back to the mills.

The generations, looping backwards forever. As baseball reporter Alison Gordon observed in *Foul Ball!* "I once stood outside Fenway Park in Boston, a place where the ghosts never go away, and watched a vigorous man of middle years helping, with infinite care, a frail and elderly gentleman through the milling crowds to the entry gate. Through the tears that came unexpectedly to my eyes, I saw the old man strong and important forty years before, holding the hand of a confused and excited five-year-old, showing him the way. Baseball's best moments don't always happen on the field."

This book is about Rickwood Field, another place where the ghosts never go away, and also a place of resurrection and hope for a baseball future. It is the place where baseball's legends were forged in the shadows of the immense iron and steel forges down the street in Birmingham.

It is about the teams, the players, and the games that made the park famous. It is about the men who built the ballpark and the city around it. But this book is also about memories, about our shared past, about our separate past ...

And ultimately, it's about fathers and sons.

Joseph Hersey Woodward, the industrialist multimillionaire of early Birmingham, never threw a baseball with his son. In fact, he tried to discourage his son's love of the game, which he blamed for ruining the son's grades at college. J.H. Woodward wanted his son to be serious, to be the very model of the early 20th century capitalist baron. But A.H. "Rick" Woodward loved baseball, and bought a baseball club and built a baseball park in spite of his father. He became a different kind of Baron—Head Baron of the Birmingham Barons Baseball Club, a position he would hold for over a quarter of a century. And in the process, he won over his own father, who purchased the bonds of his son's newly built stadium and became a boisterous season-ticket holder.

Here, then, is the story of Rickwood Field: for Rick Woodward, who loved the game and his city enough to defy his father; for Willie Mays Sr., who helped his son live a father's dreams; for William Putnam, who gave his grandson the gift of the memory of a Stan Musial homer; and for all the fathers and sons of Birmingham who remember, as Thomas Wolfe (a one-time batboy for a Southern minor league team) did, "the smell of the wooden bleachers in a small-town baseball park, that resinous, sultry and exciting smell of old dry wood."

It's been a pleasure updating the story of Rickwood with ballpark expert Joe Mock. We hope reading this will forge some memories of your own.

CHAPTER 1

A NEW GAME FOR THE NEW SOUTH

Professional baseball arrived in Birmingham in 1885, just five years after Alice No. 1, the district's first blast furnace, signaled the beginning of an explosive (albeit belated) industrial revolution in Alabama. Boomtown Birmingham, whose muddy streets and rude buildings presented a frontier-like appearance, held a franchise in the original Southern League, founded and presided over by Henry Grady, the Atlanta newspaperman who invented the concept of the "New South."

Grady, a true visionary, recognized the growing importance of baseball in American life, and acted to make the South a player in the great national game. The Southern League of Professional Baseball Clubs had Henry Grady's ink-stained fingerprints all over it. Grady loved promoting the Southern region to Northern businessmen and Northern money, and he also loved sports with the steadfast devotion of a child. Grady had played baseball at the University of Georgia and acquired a reputation as an aggressive, speedy base runner, not unlike a latter-day Georgian named Ty Cobb. This new league, consisting of cities south of the Ohio River with populations of 25,000 or greater, enabled Grady to combine his avocation (baseball) with his vocation (as spokesman of the "New South") in a delightful way.

Birmingham joined Atlanta, Chattanooga, Macon, Columbus (Georgia), Augusta, Nashville, and Memphis as charter members of the first professional league in the Deep South. All but Macon still host pro baseball today. Birmingham played its games at a park in North Smithfield, on the Pratt City streetcar line, where the cars were pulled by steam locomotives. There, on May 29, 1885,

Charlie Parsons, who would later pitch in the major leagues for the Boston Beaneaters, hurled the first no-hitter in Dixie. By 1887, the team had moved to Lakeside Park on Birmingham's Southside. This wooden grandstand also hosted football games, including the historic first meeting between bitter rivals the University of Alabama and Auburn University in 1893.

The league had troubles from the get-go. Players generally had to be imported from the North, as the game was too new to the South for much local talent to have emerged on local diamonds. These "Yankee" ballplayers were not dependable, often skipping town to make more money with teams in Northern circuits. Teams in cities such as Memphis and New Orleans often found themselves sidelined by the Yellow Fever epidemics that plagued the Mississippi Delta in the 1880s.

Attendance in the original Southern League was poor, but the fans exhibited a spirit that foreshadowed the rabid support Southern athletic teams were to receive in the 20th and 21st centuries. *The Atlanta Constitution* reported on a game between Atlanta and Montgomery in the 1880s in which Atlanta fans, protesting a call against their team, rushed the field "not with pop bottles, but sticks and knives and guns." Montgomery players, fearing for their lives, noted that the fans "weren't only after the umpire. They were after us. They looked on visiting players as their natural enemies." Henry Grady, at the game to cover it for *The Constitution* (in addition to being the first Southern League president, he was the first baseball writer in Dixie) quelled the riot by appealing to the sportsmanship of the mob. Two minutes after threatening the lives of umpires and opponents, the crowd was quietly seated in the Atlanta grandstand.

Grady died in December 1889, and the baseball league he founded died with him. The league resumed play in 1892 with Birmingham taking its first pennant. However, play remained sporadic (two years––1897 and 1898–had no baseball) until 1901, when the Southern Association began its sixty-year run. This legendary league, organized at meetings in Birmingham in October and November of 1900, is the league of Barons and Crackers, of Pelicans and Chicks, of Lookouts and Vols—the league fondly remembered by generations of fans raised before television and air conditioning. The Southern Association was the loop that mattered to the serious baseball fan in Dixie.

The earliest Southern Association games in Birmingham were played at what was formally known as West End Park. The locals never called it that, though. To them, it was the Slag Pile.

The Slag Pile consisted of a crude wooden grandstand that supposedly seated 600. Freeloading fans sat on piles of slag outside the outfield fence, enabling them to see the action while giving the ballpark an enduring name. The Tennessee Coal, Iron and Railroad Company owned the land that the Slag Pile occupied and leased it to the team owners, sixty days at a time. To Birmingham fans, the ramshackle ballpark quickly came to symbolize the ramshackle organization that ran baseball in the Magic City.

Birmingham's teams fared poorly in their first decade of competition in the Southern Association. From 1901 to 1909, the clubs had losing records in six seasons. Only once did the home team bring home a pennant. That was the 1906 club, called the Vulcanites. The nickname Barons, a shortened version of Coal Barons, came into accepted use soon afterward.

Most Birmingham ball clubs from this era were considered an embarrassment to the city. In a sentiment carried forward by generations of sports fans to come, the local partisans blamed apathetic, tightfisted ownership. Their assessment was simple: cheap ballpark, cheap players, cheap owner. The fans wanted an owner who would spend money and bring in some quality talent ... and perhaps spend enough to give the fans a decent place to sit during the game. In short, Birmingham's baseball community longed for a "classy" owner, one willing to give the city a team and a ballpark worthy of its stature.

Rumors swirled as the winter of 1909-10 descended on the city. A wealthy young man wanted the Barons for his own—a young man who loved baseball and was willing to spend serious money to obtain a winner for Birmingham. And the rumors included another tantalizing prospect: the new owner had committed himself to building a new ballpark, the finest in the minor leagues.

CHAPTER 2

THE NAME ABOVE THE GATE

Birmingham in 1910 was a city adolescent in nature. Energetic and optimistic, growing at an exponential rate, the city looked to a golden future seemingly assured by its industrial importance to the South and the nation. Young Birmingham, only thirty-nine years old in 1910, boasted a population of 132,685, an increase of over 90,000 people since the dawn of the 20th century. Somewhat awkward and unruly, often wild and undisciplined, it was a city best described as smart, inventive, and clever rather than wise. Wisdom would come later, after hard lessons and hard times, both economically and socially.

The years before the Great War belonged more to the 19th century than the 20th. Europe still genuflected before monarchs seated on ancient thrones. Edward VII of Great Britain, old and paunchy, reigned over an empire comprising one-sixth of the world. His nephew Nicholas II, the last Czar of Russia, ruled another one-sixth, while another nephew, Kaiser Wilhelm II of Germany, held a substantial portion of the remainder of the globe.

American royalty was of a different form. The great capitalist barons, the makers of great fortunes like the Carnegies, the Rockefellers, and the Morgans, were the nobles of the New World. In a nation without a hereditary aristocracy, the rich became the revered symbols of the nation's strength and importance. In early 20th-century America, before the Great Depression and a sea change in American ideals, the captains of industry were idols, heroes, the Great Men whose deeds defined the United States to the world.

In Birmingham, the Great Men were the pioneer developers and industrialists who had turned an obscure railroad intersection into the industrial center of the region and one of the great steel-making cities of the world. Their surnames were known by even the poorest inhabitants of the region: DeBardeleben, Jemison, Linn, and Woodward. The coal-and-iron magnate DeBardeleben, the land mogul Jemison, the banker Linn, the iron master Woodward—these men held great power in the minds of early Birmingham. They had created the city out of fire and dust, blast furnace and iron ore. These men were the Wizards of the Magic City. Birmingham looked to its capitalists for leadership.

Joseph Hersey Woodward, Founder of Woodward Iron Company, largest pig iron producer in the world

Joseph Hersey Woodward was sixty-six years old in 1910. He had first arrived in the Birmingham area in the 1870s, sent by his father, Stimpson Hersey Woodward, an Ohio Valley iron manufacturer, to inspect iron-ore-rich properties the elder Woodward had shrewdly purchased in 1869. Along with his brother, William H. Woodward, Joe Woodward founded the Woodward Iron Company in 1881. By 1886, control of the company rested solely in the hands of Joseph Hersey Woodward, where it would remain until the old iron master breathed his last in 1917.

J.H. Woodward was not a self-made man. He had arrived in Birmingham with $400,000 in cash from his father to establish an iron works. But Joe Woodward created an empire far greater than his father's LaBelle Iron Works in Wheeling, West Virginia, through single-minded hard work and conservative business practices. Woodward refused to speculate in an age of speculation. "Slow, steady, legitimate development work was Joe Woodward's motto; No booming no fireworks no talk," said *The Birmingham News* about the no-nonsense businessman.

Unlike other Birmingham business leaders of his time, Joe lived simply. Instead of building an ostentatious mansion, Woodward bought the old home of Colonel Jacob Sloss, another Birmingham iron man, for his family. There he lived a reclusive life. "Very few people even saw him," noted *The News*.

Just about everyone, however, saw Joseph Hersey Woodward's only son and heir. Christened Allan Harvey Woodward at his birth in Wheeling in 1876, "Rick" Woodward lived a life of sport and song that inevitably brought conflict with his straitlaced father. When Rick Woodward returned from a seven-year adventure at two colleges (the University of the South and the Massachusetts Institute of Technology) where he earned low marks in scholarship but high marks as a bon vivant, he was behind the wheel of the first automobile in Birmingham. Rick hunted big game in exotic locales. He played at being a locomotive engineer. His name frequently appeared in the newspapers.

Joe Woodward was disgusted. His son, to his way of thinking, was behaving in a degenerate manner. And Joe Woodward knew what had caused his son's decline.

Baseball.

Allan Harvey "Rick" Woodward, the man who built Rickwood Field

Young Rick had been hooked by the game when his uncle had taken him to see major league stars, on their way north after spring training, play exhibitions at the old Lakeview Park in Birmingham. Rick joined the baseball team in college, where he became a catcher, launching a lifelong fascination with catching pitched baseballs. As his interest in the game soared, his grades dropped. Joe Woodward, who had made a fortune by spotting trends, noticed the correlation between sports and academics as it pertained to the future head of the Woodward Iron Company. He brought the boy home.

A second go at college (B.S. in Mining Engineering, MIT, '99) went better for young Rick, and perhaps Joe rested a bit easier. Baseball had been a youthful folly for his son, nothing more—or so the elder Woodward hoped. Now Rick would learn the iron business from the ground up. Joe Woodward believed in hard lessons.

Rick Woodward found his life after college far different from the sporting days he had so enjoyed during his first sojourn in higher education. He worked as a leather wrapper at the Woodward Furnaces—hard, hot, sweaty work. Joe knew that the brutal experience would pay off when Rick took over the company.

What Joe did not know was that he had inadvertently reintroduced Rick to baseball. Soon, the younger Woodward took the field again, playing with other workers after their shifts at the furnaces were finished. Eventually, Rick became, as he put it, "a sort of proprietor of a manufacturing team, and a good one it was." Rick's team won its way into a championship game for manufacturing teams, to be played at West End Park.

But Rick learned a hard lesson at the Slag Pile that day. His players, all fellow employees of the Woodward Iron Company, had been making demands of the young proprietor in the days before the championship game. They asked for winter clothes, new shoes, bonuses, and assorted other goodies that Rick refused to provide. In the championship game, Rick watched as his once-powerful charges were slaughtered. During the game, Rick heard several of his players laughing at him under their breath. In a foreshadowing of events to unfold on the South Side of Chicago in 1919, Rick's players had gotten even with him for refusing their demands.

As the sun set on his defeat, Rick knew what he wanted. He wanted a baseball team—a real team, a team of professionals, one that he would pay a fair dollar, and from whom he could expect a fair effort in return. Rick Woodward had the itch, and only one thing would soothe him: the local baseball franchise, the Birmingham Barons of the Southern Association.

Joe was apoplectic. He wanted his son to stay out of baseball. He feared for his son's business career and for the well-being and success of the Woodward Iron Company itself. The elder Woodward, stone-deaf for a number of years, now required the services of two nurses due to a degenerative heart condition. He surmised he wouldn't live much longer, and he fretted that his son was still too immature and frivolous to handle the family company.

Rick, unswayed by his father's concerns, pursued his dream. In late 1909, before leaving for the Woodward family winter home in Orlando, Rick Woodward offered J. Williams McQueen, the majority owner of the Birmingham Barons baseball club, $20,000 for his share of the team, representing about two-thirds of the stock. On January 24, 1910, Rick got the answer his father dreaded: Rick now owned a controlling interest in the Birmingham Barons, which he would hold for twenty-eight seasons.

In Rick Woodward, Birmingham baseball had a leader who had grown up with the city. Young (only thirty-three), confident to the point of arrogance, with values and beliefs unquestioned and untested, he personified the city to which he would *be* baseball for the next quarter of a century.

CHAPTER 3

"AS NEAR PERFECT AS SKILL AND MONEY COULD MAKE IT"

Cornelius Alexander McGillicuddy, better known by his baseball moniker Connie Mack, wanted a new ballpark for the 1909 season. He managed and was a part owner of the popular Philadelphia Athletics of the American League. Mr. Mack's team played at Columbia Park, a wooden structure that could accommodate about 12,000 fans. Knowing he could sell the additional tickets if majority owner Ben Shibe gave him the additional seats, Mack proposed a bold course of action. The Athletics would not simply add to Columbia Park or build another wooden grandstand. Instead, Shibe and Mack planned a new kind of baseball stadium, constructed entirely of concrete and steel.

Shibe Park, which opened on April 12, 1909, with the Athletics defeating the Boston Red Sox, 8-1, before 30,162 fans, was the first of a second generation of ballparks. Between 1909 and 1915, twelve new arenas were built in the majors, all featuring concrete-and-steel construction throughout. These new ballfields, including Forbes Field in Pittsburgh (which opened only eleven weeks after Shibe Park), Fenway Park in Boston, Navin Field (later Tiger Stadium) in Detroit, Ebbets Field in Brooklyn, and Weeghman Field (now Wrigley Field) in Chicago, were built to last—to withstand the elements, to retard fire, to resist rotting. In 1950, for example, all twelve of the second-generation ballparks were still standing, and eleven still hosted Major League Baseball. Unlike the wooden grandstands they replaced, these sturdy structures reflected the stability of the franchises and the commitment of the owners.

Professional baseball was a permanent fixture in urban American life. The solidly built, beautiful new venues emphasized that permanence.

"Incorporating steel and concrete not only ushered in ballparks with larger capacities, bigger upper seating decks, and the ability to sell more tickets, it grew the game and legitimized professional baseball," noted Jason Michael Ford, principal at sports-architecture powerhouse Populous. "This new wave of ballparks was considered permanent, safer, and not as susceptible to fire."

The latter factor was particularly significant.

The Boston Braves' South End Grounds burned down in 1894, as did Sportsman's Park in St. Louis in 1898, League Park in Cincinnati in 1900, and two in 1911—American League Park in Washington and New York's Polo Grounds. All had been built of wood.

Clearly, wood was no longer the way to go in ballpark construction, and Connie Mack knew it.

This second generation of ballparks represented a transitional period in stadium architecture. Until this time, the very names of ballparks reflected the rural origins of the sport ... and of America itself. Every park built in the majors from 1909 until Yankee Stadium was completed in 1923 included "Field," "Grounds," or "Park" in its name, even if the ballfield sat smack in the middle of a bustling urban neighborhood. When the New York Yankees' "The House That Ruth Built" adopted the more grandiose sobriquet of "Stadium," it marked the triumph of the urban milieu in baseball—the stadium as skyscraper.

The excitement created by the opening of Shibe Park and Forbes Field did not escape the notice of an interested observer in Birmingham. Rick Woodward had decided, even before closing his purchase of the Birmingham Barons, that a new grandstand for the team was a necessity. Immediately after taking control in January 1910, Woodward announced plans for the construction of a ballpark—a steel-and-concrete ballpark, the first in the minor leagues and only the fifth ever built, as League Park in Cleveland and Comiskey Park in Chicago had opened early in 1910.

Woodward had toured the original big-league concrete-and-steel parks looking for inspiration. In Philadelphia, Connie Mack took an interest in the young owner and his project. When Mack brought his Athletics to play an exhibition game against the Barons in Birmingham in March 1910, Woodward excitedly escorted Mack to the chosen site for his new ballpark. No doubt the young Woodward was seeking the advice and probably the approval of baseball royalty.

Mack gladly obliged by guiding the layout of a baseball diamond on the construction site, orienting the field in the same way as Shibe Park, to diminish the sun as a factor in fielding. When Woodward pointed out that the afternoon sun was particularly harsh during Birmingham's summers, Mack is said to have suggested the installation of wooden louvers between the top row of the grandstand and the roof. These louvers were angled to block the western sun as it submerged behind the billowing smokestacks during late-afternoon innings but still allowed fresh air to circulate through the grandstand.

It is also apparent that Connie Mack had something to do with the new park's dimensions. The distances to the fences were remarkably similar to those at Shibe Park, and the distance from home plate to the backstop at Rickwood—at ninety feet, it was a catcher's dream for chasing down foul pop-ups—matched Shibe precisely. The new ballpark in Birmingham, as constructed, features a layout with a grandstand flanked by two symmetrical bleachers similar to Shibe Park. The influence that Connie Mack had on the design of Rickwood Field is impossible to determine precisely, but the final design of the Birmingham ballpark appears to owe at least as much to his Shibe Park as to Forbes Field, the more frequently cited "model" for the stadium.

Even before Rickwood Field was constructed, published reports claimed that the Birmingham ballpark had been patterned after Forbes Field. When the grandstand plans were publicly unveiled in March 1910—only one week after Connie Mack had consulted with Woodward—*The Birmingham Age-Herald* stated that the blueprints for the park had been drawn by the "southern representative of the General Fireproofing Company, designers and builders of the grandstand at Forbes Field." Despite such repeated assertions of local media outlets, however, no definitive link between the designers and builders of Forbes Field (architect Charles W. Leavitt Jr. and Nicola Construction Company) and the men credited with the plans for Rickwood (the Southeastern Engineering Company) has ever been established.

One tantalizing tidbit does link Rick Woodward to Leavitt, though. When Woodward built a palatial mansion atop Birmingham's Red Mountain a few years after Rickwood Field had been completed, Leavitt designed the estate's grounds.

The Southeastern Engineering Company, whose name appears on the plans for Rickwood Field, sprang into existence only weeks before construction of the ballpark began. Josiah Hubert Scruggs, the senior partner of the firm, had been a boyhood friend of Rick Woodward. Prior to forming Southeastern Engineering, he had worked as a salesman for the Woodward Lumber Company. Although he had two years of engineering training at the University of Texas, it is unlikely that young Scruggs possessed the expertise at this point in his career to handle the design work on a project as large as Rickwood Field. His partner, Eugene Morrison, had worked as an engineer for the Southern Bridge Company and probably did the technical "heavy lifting" on the Rickwood project.

It is possible, perhaps probable, that another man with engineering knowledge and experience took a leading role in the preparation of the Rickwood blueprints: Rick Woodward. He had more engineering training and experience than Scruggs. In addition to his engineering degree from MIT, he held patents for a number of industrial machines he designed during the early 1900s while working in technical supervision for the Woodward Iron Company. Given the intimacy of his association with the ballpark project, his stated desire to build a first-class facility, and his engineering background, Rick Woodward is the one person who probably deserves the most credit for the design of Rickwood Field.

The original plans for Rickwood called for a concrete-and-steel, single-deck, roofed grandstand wrapped around the diamond from first base to third, seating 3,000 fans. The steel-columned grandstand, forged from Birmingham Red Mountain ore, could be double-decked to make Rickwood a big-league park one day—a notion that was likely to have been in the back of Woodward's mind. The two flanking bleachers, also constructed of concrete, could accommodate 2,000 more customers. Standing room in the park would bring the official capacity to 7,000. Estimated cost for the project: $25,000.

The 1910 Southern Association season began, and Rick Woodward's attention was drawn away from stadium construction as he had a ball club to run. After a quick facelift for the Slag Pile and a promising spring-training session, the Barons assumed their customary position at the bottom of the standings by the end of April. Fans who had expected better from the new ownership clamored for action. Woodward, despite construction cost overruns that had strapped his resources, decided that players—preferably major league players—had to be obtained, and that he would pay the price demanded.

Woodward bought pitcher Harry Coveleski from the Cincinnati Reds for $1,000, then purchased switch-hitting (and lightly used) outfielder Bobby Messenger from the Chicago White Sox for a second $1,000. By the standards of the day, the purchases represented reckless wheeling-and-dealing by a minor league owner. However, Woodward's judgment proved sound. Messenger, an experienced player, performed well for the Barons, and Coveleski's performance in the summer of 1910 was nothing short of phenomenal.

Branded by many as a "big-league washout," Harry Coveleski came to Birmingham hoping to rebuild a once-promising career. In 1908, the young southpaw (only twenty-two) beat the New York Giants three times in September as John McGraw's charges blew the pennant by one game. "Giant Killer" Coveleski became a national figure, mentioned in the same breath as the great Christy Mathewson. But the Harry Coveleski who arrived in Birmingham in 1910 had lost eleven of his previous eighteen decisions, along with a goodly portion of his confidence.

He started slowly in Birmingham, losing his first several decisions. As the summer wore on, he began to regain his form. Coveleski pitched a no-hitter on July 17, although he lost the game in extra innings. He hurled a second no-no two weeks later. Down the stretch, he won 11 consecutive games, allowing only 17 runs over the course of his streak. By August, the Barons, buoyed by the success of their ace, were in third place, just eight games back of the front-running New Orleans Pelicans.

As the Barons contended for a pennant, their new home park approached completion. Rickwood's price tag had soared to $75,000, straining Rick Woodward's finances to a critical point. The young owner had insisted on lofty standards throughout construction, and the resulting cost overruns now threatened his entire operation. Woodward set the opening of his ballpark for August 18, and he hoped that the venue would draw the big paying crowds he needed to make his investment pay off.

This ballpark, like Shibe Park and Comiskey Park, would be named for its builder. However, instead of the obvious "Woodward Park" or "Woodward Field," the name selected in a newspaper contest (contrary to popular legend, Rick Woodward did *not* name the ballyard after himself) involved a combination and contraction of Rick Woodward's name: Rickwood. In the early days, "Rickwood Field" and "Rickwood Park" were used interchangeably to refer to the facility. Gradually, "Field" won out over "Park" as the more popular designation.

"There is no doubt but that Birmingham is 'baseball wild,'" declared *The Birmingham Age-Herald* on the eve of Rickwood's opening. City businesses announced a half-holiday for the 18th, closing their doors at 3 p.m. so that no one would have to miss the glorious spectacle of the inaugural game at Birmingham's new baseball palace. "The new ballpark opens tomorrow. Most all PATRIOTIC Birmingham folk will be there," lectured an advertisement by a clothier.

Rickwood had already garnered laudatory reviews from the local media. "In every detail, it is modern and as near perfect as skill and money could make it," trumpeted *The Birmingham Age-Herald.* "Visitors here from cities of the North and East pronounce it little short of the finest among the major-league plants, and unequaled by any outside of the big leagues." *The Birmingham News* was not surprised by the grandeur of the ballpark. "When Birmingham men do a thing, they do it right."

And what the Birmingham men did was to build a stunningly sturdy ballpark. "It's no coincidence that Rickwood Field is the oldest existing professional baseball park in the United States," noted modern-day architect Ford. "It's obvious that its grandstands were inspired by Forbes Field's and Shibe Park's concrete-and-steel construction."

Rick Woodward had wrangled a schedule change from the moguls of the Southern Association, obtaining home games against the Montgomery Climbers for the dates immediately following Rickwood's scheduled completion. His construction schedule almost proved too ambitious, however, as carpenters were still working on the bleachers as the crowd gathered for the opening game. A steamroller rumbled over the grassless infield until the players took the field.

Rickwood Field on Opening Day, August 18, 1910

In the early afternoon, the fans arrived in force. They overflowed the grandstand, the bleachers, and the standing room as well. Part of the playing field was roped off for spectators. The throng, conservatively estimated at 10,000, approached the all-time Southern Association attendance record.

At 3:30 p.m. on August 18, 1910, Rick Woodward threw the first pitch at Rickwood Field. He did *not* throw out a ceremonial first pitch. No, in typical Woodwardian fashion, he took the field with the Barons and appeared in the game as the first pitcher ever at Rickwood. His one heave delivered (and called ball one by the umpire), Woodward retired to the owner's box, handing the ball over to Harry Coveleski.

The game came remarkably close to living up to the ballyhoo that surrounded it. Playing manager Carleton Molesworth of the Barons scored the first run in the new park. Derrill "Del" Pratt of the Climbers, perhaps the most famous athlete produced by the state of Alabama up to that time (due to his football exploits at the University of Alabama), played a fine game, getting two hits and driving in a run. Coveleski, as usual, was superb, allowing only two runs over nine innings. But the Barons still trailed, 2-1, as they picked up their bats for the bottom of the ninth.

The Barons, urged on by their hot, tired, but still boisterous fans, pulled it out. The leadoff Baron was hit by a pitch by Bill Duggleby, the old Climber pitcher who had once been a fine major leaguer for the Philadelphia Phillies. Barons manager Molesworth then ordered four straight bunts, which produced one out and the winning two runs, squeezed home by taps off the bats of infielders Roy Ellam and Lou Emory.

As the crowd thundered its approval, an elderly man of means who had never liked baseball found himself on his feet, shouting for joy in a most undignified manner. The old gentleman then joined a happy throng of fans as they exited Rickwood Field and headed east to their homes. As the old man reached his house on Highland Avenue, he knew that Rick Woodward had done a fine thing, and he resolved to help the young man with his financial difficulties. Baseball must be encouraged. It was a great game, he thought, good for the spirit of the people, good for the morale of the working men. The old man decided to purchase the bonds of the ballpark and retire Rickwood Field's debt, ensuring Rick Woodward's success.

Having made up his mind, Joseph Hersey Woodward retired for the evening.

CHAPTER 4

"BENEATH A HALO OF INCOMPARABLE GLORY"

The Birmingham Barons finished the 1910 Southern Association season in second place, just ahead of the hated Atlanta Crackers. The pennant went to the New Orleans Pelicans, a team with a number of ancient ex-big leaguers (pitcher Theodore Breitenstein had registered 160 wins in the majors—but none of them in the 20th century!) and one young prospect whom the Philadelphia Athletics had given up on. That prospect was an illiterate outfielder from South Carolina with the incongruously theatrical name of Joseph Jefferson Jackson. Teammates in the low minors had hung a more appropriate title on the rural innocent: "Shoeless Joe."

Joe Jackson turned twenty-one that summer of 1910, and he turned the Southern Association on its ear. The league had never seen a more dominant player. Even Tris Speaker, the Little Rock star of 1908, paled in comparison. Shoeless Joe's .355 batting average outpaced runner-up Bill McGilvray of the Barons by a whopping thirty-one percentage points as Jackson captured the loop batting crown. The big (6'1", 200 lbs.) Pelican outfielder hit for power as well as average, and he was unquestionably the finest fielder in the league.

The pennant-winning Pelicans made their only appearance at Rickwood on September 7, 1910. The game marked the close of the Barons' home schedule, and Birmingham fans packed the park for one last look at baseball before the season's curtain fell.

They got an eyeful. Harry Coveleski, pitching for the final time in Birmingham, won his 11th straight game (and his 21st overall) by shutting out the Pelicans, 1-0. Coveleski held Jackson hitless, but Shoeless Joe still managed to electrify the crowd.

In the seventh inning, with two out and nobody on base, Lil Marcan of the Barons smacked a line drive to deep right center field. New Orleans right fielder Hyder Barr drew a bead on the ball and appeared capable of making the play when Joe Jackson, streaking out of center field, took matters into his own hands. Jackson called Barr off the play and proceeded to make a spectacular catch at full gallop. Then Jackson stopped suddenly, turned on his heel, and threw the ball all the way across the field and into the bleachers along the left-field side of the park.

"The throw was from the scoreboard in deep right center," marveled *The Birmingham News*. "The pellet hurtled along at splendid speed, passed the diamond 50 feet in the air and plunged without checking itself amid the bleachers."

"It was the most marvelous throw ever witnessed in Birmingham, and preceded by the one-hand running catch, the entire exhibition was as spectacular as was ever seen in Birmingham."

The News stopped gushing about Jackson's feat long enough to issue a warning that, in light of later events, seems remarkably prescient: "But at the same time one became impressed with the belief that in order to stand before the throng of people beneath a halo of incomparable glory, he was willing to run the risk of dropping the ball which would have sent a runner to third."

Ten years to the month after his heroics at Rickwood Field, Shoeless Joe Jackson was indicted for his role in the Black Sox scandal, in which Jackson and seven of his Chicago White Sox teammates stood accused of conspiring to throw the 1919 World Series. Jackson, at the zenith of a storied major league career, was accused of accepting cash from gamblers eager to make money betting on the Series. But even though Jackson *seemed* willing to throw the Series, he could not bring himself to look bad. He hit .375 in the fall classic and played errorless ball in the field. In the end, the championship of the baseball world for Chicago and the White Sox had not meant as much to Joe Jackson as did his personal reputation as a premier ballplayer.

In the early years of the 20th century, Birmingham often served as a spring training site for big-league clubs. Before the construction of Rickwood, manager John McGraw brought his New York Giants to Birmingham to round into shape for the upcoming season. The Giants soon wore out their welcome in the Magic City, however. Christy Mathewson, the great pitcher for the Giants, apparently was shocked by the number of prostitutes in Birmingham, and the squeaky-clean hurler communicated his disgust to the media. The Giants further angered locals when they allegedly told New York sportswriters that Birmingham residents enjoyed a unique "sport" that involved chasing Black people with bloodhounds. The situation eventually became so untenable for McGraw and his men that the Giants were forced to sneak out of Birmingham by night, long before the scheduled end of their spring training stay.

Rick Woodward's spanking-new facility spurred fresh interest in Birmingham as a major league training site. The Philadelphia Phillies jumped at the opportunity to hold spring workouts at Rickwood Field in 1911.

The Philadelphia franchise of the National League had competed for twenty-eight seasons without winning a single pennant. As spring practice opened in Birmingham in March 1911, catcher/manager Charlie "Red" Dooin hoped to find a championship team hidden somewhere in the midst of the Phillies veterans and rookie recruits working out on the grass of Rickwood Field.

In truth, everything that the Phillies needed to end decades of futility shuffled to and from the Rickwood pitcher's mound every day, barely noticed by Dooin. In fact, there was little about Grover Cleveland Alexander that suggested anything other than sloth. He never seemed in a hurry to get anywhere, an unusual trait for a rookie supposedly trying to impress the coaches with hustle. His ill-fitting uniform looked as if it had been slept in (which, given the pitcher's fondness for spirits after a workout, was a plausible explanation). And worst of all, his nonchalance struck the Phillies coaches as indolence. Unimpressed with the rookie's live fastball and wicked curve, Dooin decided to leave Alexander in Birmingham with the Barons, as a way of thanking Rick Woodward for the use of his ballpark.

Pat Moran, a Phillies coach as well as Dooin's backup at catcher, pleaded for Alexander. "Let the kid come north with me on the second squad, Red," Moran begged, "and I'll have a pitcher for you when we get back home." Dooin agreed, and when the first and second Phillies squads met in Philadelphia after completing barnstorming tours of the East Coast, Moran told Dooin that Alexander was ready for the big leagues. "He's a pitcher if ever I saw one," Moran insisted.

Pat Moran was right. Grover Cleveland Alexander won 28 games for the Phillies in 1911, the most ever by a rookie pitcher. During his twenty-year career in the National League, Alexander posted 373 wins, matching Christy Mathewson's all-time league record. "Old Pete" Alexander tossed 90 shutouts, a National League record and second on the all-time list. And in 1915, with Pat Moran managing, Alexander pitched the Phillies to the National League pennant, the only flag the Phillies would win prior to 1950.

The permanent inhabitants of Rickwood Field, the Birmingham Barons, reclaimed exclusive rights to their turf after the Phillies departed in late March 1911. Rick Woodward's second club finished third in the Southern Association, slightly off the pace of the previous year's team. In 1912, however, long-suffering Birmingham fans cheered the first pennant winner to call Rickwood Field home.

CHAPTER 5

YOUNG STUBBLEBEARD

Carleton Molesworth, manager and sometime infielder for the Birmingham Barons, knew that the 1912 season could very well be his last in the Magic City. Barons fans attending the previous season's Fourth of July doubleheader at Rickwood had answered a pollster's query of "should Moley manage the Barons in 1912?" with a resounding "no." Even under the best of circumstances, Rick Woodward possessed the patience of a child on Christmas Eve. When the Barons fell to third in the Southern Association in 1911 (after 1910's second-place finish), the young owner was beside himself. Molesworth began to feel the weight of Woodward's stare—not just at a distance but from close range since Woodward habitually sat on the Barons bench (wearing a team uniform!) during home games at Rickwood. Perhaps because of Woodward's presence on the bench (or perhaps because Molesworth was too short to see out of the dugout while seated), Molesworth did his managing from a cane-back chair positioned outside the dugout.

The two men were natural enemies. Molesworth was a rough-and-tumble ballplayer, while Woodward was a child of privilege, heir to a great fortune. Molesworth did not like "college boys," and Rick Woodward, he of the seven-year undergraduate odyssey, was the archetypical monied Big Man on Campus. The fiery manager considered his young boss a snooty, snotty know-it-all who insisted upon horning in on the managing of the Barons by making "suggestions" to Molesworth during games. For his part, Woodward judged Molesworth to be a has-been career busher with no big-league experience, not capable of meeting the lofty standards the new ownership had set for the franchise.

Original Rickwood Entry Gate, circa 1917

A hustling young outfielder from Tennessee salvaged the working relationship between Woodward and Molesworth by leading the Barons to an improbable pennant. Jimmy Johnston was small (5'10", 160 lbs.), not too fast (playing with the Brooklyn Dodgers in 1917, he was thrown out on 19 of 41 stolen base attempts), and he lacked power. But the determined Johnston made things happen on the diamond. Using quickness and baserunning savvy, he stole 81 bases for the 1912 Barons, setting a Southern Association record that outlasted the league itself. Johnston also led the league in runs scored, and he excelled in center field. Following its scrappy leader, a Barons team short on stars claimed the Southern title by virtue of a late-season four-game sweep of second-place Mobile.

Johnston eventually fought his way up to the big leagues, where he became a fan favorite in Ebbets Field for his scrappy play as a Dodgers utility man. He posted a respectable .294 career batting average over thirteen major league seasons while playing every infield and outfield position. In 1928, at age thirty-eight, he returned to the Barons, for whom he hit .338 as Birmingham won the league pennant again.

Carleton Molesworth piloted the Barons to a second flag for Rickwood in 1914. Strong pitching carried the team. The staff boasted a pair of 20-game winners in Curly Brown and Omer Hardgrove. In fact, a talented young pitcher (only twenty years old in the spring of 1914) was forced to spend almost all of his season in the Virginia League due to the depth of Barons moundsmen. Proud young Burleigh Grimes, who had been good enough to pitch in the Southern Association for Chattanooga in 1913, did not take his 1914 demotion well.

Burleigh Grimes Departs for Major League Trial, Birmingham Age-Herald

Grimes wanted to be a big leaguer. In March 1914, he loudly proclaimed his intention to jump to the new Federal League, a third major league that operated briefly during the 1910s. Grimes believed that his live fastball and hard-breaking spitball were big-league pitches. The young pitcher pinned a sarcastic letter to Barons management, essentially informing Rick Woodward that Burleigh Grimes was through with the bushes; the Barons could take their contract offer and ... give it to somebody else.

Baseball offers many proofs of the existence of a Greater Intelligence. Perhaps Rick Woodward's thoughts in the spring of 1914 were of a benevolent providence as Burleigh Grimes, whose Federal League deal had fallen through, worked out at Rickwood Field. Reporting to the Barons for spring training was an odious task for Grimes, but as Opening Day approached, his twenty-year-old ego took another direct hit. The Barons cut him from the team.

Sent down to Richmond, a determined Grimes set to work rebuilding his foundering career. He won 23 games for Richmond, striking out 190 batters in 296 innings of work. It was an impressive season, one that easily won the righthander a promotion to Birmingham in 1915.

Barons teammates quickly noticed a change in Grimes from the previous year. The hard-throwing pitcher had matured. Always combative and mercurial, Grimes had learned to control his emotions on the mound. He'd become a complete pitcher, one who captured the notice of a baseball immortal who paid a visit to Rick Woodward just prior to the 1915 season. Honus Wagner, after watching Grimes warm up in the Birmingham sun, told his friend Rick that the young righthander was going to be great.

The Flying Dutchman couldn't have been more correct.

For the first month of the 1915 Southern Association season, Grimes was the most dominant force the Barons had ever unleashed on the league. He started the season hot and only got hotter. He did not allow an earned run in his first 24 innings of work in 1915, and in his first 60 innings he struck out 42 batters (a great ratio in the dead-ball era) to lead the league. Knowledgeable fans in Birmingham began to discuss Burleigh's chances of winning 30 games for the Barons. After a particularly impressive three-hit shutout of the Memphis Chicks in Rickwood on May 9, *The Birmingham Age-Herald* shouted in the headline what Southern Association batters had known for weeks: "Burleigh Grimes is invincible!"

Immediately after his gem in Rickwood, however, Grimes found out he was not invincible against every foe. An attack of the mumps took him out of the pitching rotation for seventeen days. When he returned, his performances were erratic for several weeks. He would not truly regain his pre-mumps form until late in the 1915 season, and the Barons fell to second in the Southern's pennant race.

Even though illness had taken away a large chunk of his 1915 season, his final numbers remained impressive. He set a Barons' single-season record of 158 strikeouts. In the next forty years only one Barons pitcher would top that mark. Grimes worked 296 innings, winning 17 games against 13 losses. His earned-run average—a brand-new stat adopted by the sport in 1913—was a sparkling 2.04.

Burleigh enjoyed an even better season in 1916. He won 20 games for Birmingham with only 11 losses, while his ERA improved a hair to 2.02. His strikeout total fell to 119, but he also allowed fewer hits and walks. And, on August 8, 1916, Burleigh Grimes realized the ambition that had driven him through two successful seasons in Birmingham: his contract was purchased from the Barons by the Pittsburgh Pirates, with a promise to call the young pitcher up for the September stretch run. After three full additional seasons in the minors, Grimes had achieved the goal that eluded him in the spring of 1914. He was a big leaguer. Not only that, it made him a teammate of Wagner, who retired the following year at the age of forty-three.

Grimes played nineteen major league seasons, winning 270 games against 212 losses, a fine .560 percentage. He made it to the Baseball Hall of Fame in Cooperstown in 1964, the second former Birmingham Baron to be honored. (Pie Traynor was first.) Although he was the finest pitcher in the National League during the 1920s (he won 190 games during that decade, more than anyone else in baseball), his great claim to fame with the fans of today is his place in baseball history as the last legal spitball picture in the big leagues.

But "Ol' Stubblebeard" Grimes (the nickname came from his refusal to shave on the days he pitched because the slippery elm he chewed to increase saliva production irritated his face) was much more than just a one-pitch wonder. A gifted athlete, a hard thrower with one of the best fastballs in the game, a good hitter, a great competitor, a man with a talent for winning—Burleigh Grimes richly deserved his place in the Hall of Fame. His record in Birmingham strongly suggests that he was the finest pitcher ever to wear a Barons uniform.

CHAPTER 6

A PUTTING AWAY OF CHILDISH THINGS

On December 15, 1917, Joseph Hersey Woodward died at his home on Highland Avenue in Birmingham, only hours before the 74th anniversary of his birth. To the end, the old iron master retained absolute control over his business interests. As the old man's heart disease entered its final stage during the fall and early winter of 1917, Rick Woodward (forty-one years old and allegedly an adult) reported to his father's sick room several times each week to receive detailed instructions for the running of the family shop. Only death could pry Joe Woodward's fingers off the short leash that chafed the neck of his independent son.

The capricious playboy now possessed the keys to the kingdom. Rick Woodward, only son and heir of the great industrialist, claimed his birthright, becoming chairman of the board of the Woodward Iron Company.

Prodded by his new responsibilities, the sporting young gentleman began to change. Even before he took over the reins of the family business, Woodward had considered selling the Barons and Rickwood Field. Banned from the Birmingham dugout for most of the 1916 season for engaging in fisticuffs with umpire Bulldog Williams in a tunnel under the stands, Woodward felt his enthusiasm for the game of his youth begin to wane. He began to spend his summer afternoons at the golf course, and local newspapers speculated about an impending retirement from baseball by the owner.

Although he ultimately decided to retain his franchise, Woodward took a less active role in the affairs of the Birmingham Barons after assuming control of Woodward Iron. The Great War, which shortened the 1918 Southern Association season to fewer than 70 games, also diverted his attentions from his baseball team. Deprived of the undivided attention and prodigious energies of its leading fan, the club became a perennial also-ran in the Southern Association. Prior to 1917, Woodward's team had placed no lower than third in the final standings. However, from 1919 to 1925, the Barons finished in the second division of the eight-team league five times.

The fine Barons teams of the 1910s had been built on the profits of the Woodward Iron Company. Joseph Hersey Woodward's genius generated the fortune that found its way into his son's pockets, and the young owner used his considerable assets to purchase the ballplayers he needed to put a winner on the field at Rickwood. Outstanding talent, led by the likes of Emil "Irish" Meusel, a lifetime .310 hitter in the majors for the Phillies and the Giants, and slick-fielding Billy Southworth (Woodward's all-time favorite Barons right fielder and a future Hall of Famer as a manager) paraded through Rickwood. But the downturn of the iron and steel industry after World War I, along with Rick's inexperience at the helm of a major corporation, resulted in financial difficulties for Woodward Iron. Naturally, this led to a decline in the quality of players suiting up for Birmingham. No longer could Woodward solve all the Barons' problems by buying the contracts of a major leaguer or two. The Birmingham nines of the early 1920s were not very talented, and the newly tightfisted owner no longer had the disposable income to buy pennant winners.

In spite of the Barons' long slump, attendance soared at Rickwood Field, with almost 200,000 fans packing the park in 1923 to watch a so-so club that ended up in fifth place. The attendance totals from 1925 showed that 182,000 paying customers made the trip to the West End to cheer for a seventh-place team that finished 18 games under .500. The attendance figures from the early 1920s are all the more impressive given the Barons did not play Sunday games and night baseball was more than a decade away.

Two factors contributed to the Barons' box office success. A great baseball boom, fueled by Babe Ruth and the "lively" ball, exploded in Jazz Age America. And Rick Woodward—while unable to obtain large numbers of star players for his team—still managed to acquire a few solid gate attractions to lure the local baseball fans to his playground.

Many of Woodward's stars came to him courtesy of the Pittsburgh Pirates of the National League, thanks to Woodward's working agreement with Pittsburgh owner Barney Dreyfuss. This allowed for the transfer of baseball talent between the two steel cities. The two men became friends when the young Birmingham owner sought out the Pirates boss for advice on ballpark construction before building Rickwood. Top Pittsburgh prospects, "farmed out" to the Barons for experience, or because of a talent stockpile at a certain position, became Rick Woodward's marquee players in the post-World War I era.

"Jughandle Johnny" Morrison, owner of one of the most knee-buckling curves in baseball history, endeared himself to Birmingham fans by winning 26 games in 1920, tying Carmen "Specs" Hill's three-year-old Barons record. Hill became better known as the first man known to have appeared in a major league game wearing glasses. Jughandle Johnny endeared himself to Birmingham speakeasy owners by becoming their best customer. Reared in the hill country of Kentucky, Morrison had a taste for the bourbon whiskey of his native sod, a taste that eventually drowned his promising career (which included a 25-win season for Pittsburgh in 1923).

Local hero Whitey Glazner of Sycamore, Alabama, won 24 games against 10 losses in '20 to team with Morrison as perhaps the best one-two pitching duo ever for the Barons. The following year, as a 27-year-old rookie, Glazner posted an impressive 14-5 record with a 2.77 ERA for the Pirates. But Whitey had left his best days behind him in the minors, and his big-league career faded quickly.

Dutch Bernsen, a power-hitting first baseman, established a remarkable Barons record by slamming 22 homers in 1921. He more than doubled the previous Barons homer record, and the new record stood for twenty years. Bernsen's seemingly modest homer total was deceptive, as Rickwood's extremely deep fences caused problems for home run hitters. No Baron *ever* topped Bernsen's mark prior to the shortening of the Rickwood fences in the 1940s. Bernsen also rapped 27 doubles and 13 triples in '21, while batting .337—one of the great power-hitting performances ever in the Southern Association.

Twenty-one-year-old Harold Traynor of Framingham, Massachusetts, proved an enormously popular drawing card for the 1921 Barons. Traynor, nicknamed "Pie" as a child after his favorite food, had appeared in 17 games at shortstop for the Pirates in 1920. Unfortunately for the hotshot prospect, 12 errors accompanied his 17 appearances in the Pirates' score book. Barney Dreyfuss decided that his club needed experience "in the hole" and traded for veteran shortstop Rabbit Maranville. Young Traynor got a train ticket to Birmingham, where the shortstop job and an uncertain future with the Pirates organization awaited him.

Pie Traynor spent only one season in a Barons uniform, but his summer of 1921 stands out in Birmingham baseball history. Traynor hit .336, with 177 hits, 101 runs, and 48 stolen bases. In spacious Rickwood he had only six homers, but his 20 doubles and 13 triples showcased the shortstop's slugging capabilities. In the field, his range and, most notably, his tremendous throwing arm impressed fan and foe alike. Years later, after decades of watching Barons stars at close range, Rick Woodward, without hesitation, named Pie Traynor the best Birmingham baseballer ever.

By the time the summer came to a close, Traynor had sparked the Barons to 90 wins, the most ever to that time by a Birmingham team. Unfortunately, that was only good enough for third place in the Southern Association that season. Still, the fans appreciated what the Barons had accomplished, and they adored their star shortstop. In fact, a special day for Pie Traynor was held at Rickwood late in the season, with gifts for Pie from the fans and a flowery tribute to the honoree written by Rick Woodward and published in *The Birmingham News*.

Traynor Day was bittersweet at Rickwood, as the Pirates had sent word to the Barons that Pie would be needed for the September stretch run. Birmingham fans knew that their star was far too good to spend a second season in the minors. Rickwood said goodbye and good luck to Pie Traynor, who headed for a big-league trial, this time showing off his arm as a third baseman.

It was at third where Traynor found a place with the Pittsburgh Pirates near the end of the 1921 season. He remained with the Pirates, manning third base, until 1937. During his long career with Pittsburgh, Traynor topped 100 RBIs on seven occasions and batted over .300 ten times. His lifetime batting average was a stunning .320. At the time of his retirement, and for many years afterward, he was universally regarded as the finest third baseman in the history of the game, giving the Pirates the distinction of having both the best third-sacker and shortstop (Honus Wagner) in the sport.

In 1948, Pie Traynor became the first Birmingham Baron inducted into Baseball's Hall of Fame in Cooperstown, New York.

As the Roaring Twenties hurtled on at breakneck speed, Rick Woodward began, once again, to intimately involve himself in the affairs of his baseball team. Woodward Iron was back on solid ground, thanks to the flush times of the postwar boom. His fortune secure, the builder of Rickwood set to work rebuilding his baseball franchise. Not satisfied with the occasional profit from renting the park for football games to the University of Alabama, Alabama Polytechnical Institute (now Auburn), or Howard College (now Samford), Woodward wanted to win at baseball, and to accomplish that end, he took the necessary steps.

Rick Woodward got out his checkbook.

CHAPTER 7

"THE FASTEST AND HARDEST BALL IN THE CIRCUIT"

Organized Black baseball in Birmingham predates the Negro Leagues. In fact, Birmingham's legacy of African-American baseball predates Rickwood Field itself.

Charles Isam Taylor arrived in Birmingham in 1904. The twenty-nine-year-old native of South Carolina had come to the South's leading boomtown to assemble a Negro baseball team. The team Taylor built and managed, the Birmingham Giants, barnstormed the South for six seasons, playing as far away from home as Chicago. The Giants played in Birmingham until 1910, when Taylor moved his entire organization to West Baden, Indiana. There, on September 11, 1911 (according to *The Birmingham Reporter,* a Black newspaper published during the 1910s, 1920s, and 1930s), the relocated Giants—now called the West Baden Sprudels—defeated the Pittsburgh Pirates of the National League, 2-1. It was the first time in baseball history that a major league team had tasted defeat at the hands of a Black team during the regular season.

Taylor eventually moved his team again, this time to Indianapolis, where the franchise became known as the Indianapolis ABCs, after the American Brewing Company, Taylor's sponsor. The ABCs were a power in early Black baseball and an original member of the Negro National League. C.I. Taylor himself helped form the league. After Andrew "Rube" Foster of the Chicago American Giants (the "Father of the Negro Leagues"), Taylor may have been the most influential figure in the early Negro Leagues. At the time of his death in 1922, Taylor was universally regarded as the finest Black manager ever. His name still appears on most lists of great Negro League managers, even as the feats of his team sink deeper into the mist of early Black baseball history.

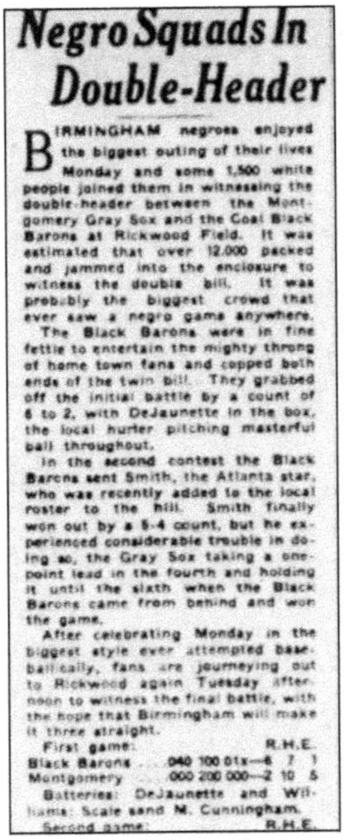

Negro Squads In Double-Header

BIRMINGHAM negroes enjoyed the biggest outing of their lives Monday and some 1,500 white people joined them in witnessing the double-header between the Montgomery Gray Sox and the Coal Black Barons at Rickwood Field. It was estimated that over 12,000 packed and jammed into the enclosure to witness the double bill. It was probably the biggest crowd that ever saw a negro game anywhere.

The Black Barons were in fine fettle to entertain the mighty throng of home town fans and copped both ends of the twin bill. They grabbed off the initial battle by a count of 6 to 2, with DeJaunette in the box, the local hurler pitching masterful ball throughout.

In the second contest the Black Barons sent Smith, the Atlanta star, who was recently added to the local roster to the hill. Smith finally won out by a 5-4 count, but he experienced considerable trouble in doing so, the Gray Sox taking a one-point lead in the fourth and holding it until the sixth when the Black Barons came from behind and won the game.

After celebrating Monday in the biggest style ever attempted baseballically, fans are journeying out to Rickwood again Tuesday afternoon to witness the final battle, with the hope that Birmingham will make it three straight.

First game:		R.	H.	E.
Black Barons	040 100 01x	6	7	1
Montgomery	000 200 000	2	10	5

Batteries: DeJaunette and Williams; Scale sand M. Cunningham.

Second game: R.H.E.

In 1919, one of the largest crowds ever to witness Black baseball crowded into Rickwood for a doubleheader

After the Birmingham Giants (who never played in Rickwood Field) moved north in 1910, Blacks in Birmingham played baseball in industrial leagues for company teams, but not in organized professional leagues. Occasionally, teams of area all-stars (with a few ringers hired on a per-game basis) played contests with Black teams from other cities at Rickwood Field. These games, usually held on holidays such as Labor Day, drew huge crowds. The estimated attendance at a Birmingham-Montgomery doubleheader in 1919 was 15,000. *The Birmingham Age-Herald* declared that "the largest crowd of negroes that had ever attended a ball game in the United States and next to the largest, irrespective of color, that ever jammed its way into Rickwood" witnessed the twin triumphs of the local squad, already called the Black Barons, by scores of 6-2 and 5-4.

Woodward's stewardship of the park during this era sometimes included the scheduling of events that stood in stark contrast to one another. He would rent his ballpark on weekends to the Black Barons in exchange for a percentage of the gate, then incongruently lease Rickwood for cross-burning rallies by the Ku Klux Klan later in the same week.

The name "Black Barons" became associated with local Black teams during the 1910s. In Birmingham, the Black team of the American Cast Iron Pipe Company (ACIPCO) was referred to as the "Black Barons" by 1919. The outstanding ACIPCO team included Negro League immortals such as George "Mule" Suttles (who was playing for ACIPCO as an eighteen-year-old in 1919). As in other

Southern cities like Atlanta, Chattanooga, and Mobile, the familiar nickname of the local white professional team eventually attached itself to the preeminent Black ballclub of the area. Thus, a dual baseball identity developed in the dual cultures of the segregated South. In Birmingham there were Black Barons and white Barons; in Chattanooga there were Black Lookouts and white Lookouts; in Mobile there were Black Bears and white Bears; and in Atlanta there were white Crackers ... and, yes, Black Crackers.

The entity identifiable by the blanket term "the Negro Leagues" was born in the YMCA at 18th and Vine in Kansas City on February 20, 1920. Rube Foster, a 6'4" former star hurler, founded the Negro National League with assistance from C.I. Taylor and a number of independent Black team owners from the Midwest. In online videos and interviews, Bob Kendrick, president of the Negro Leagues Baseball Museum, explains this story in fascinating detail.

Jonathan O'Neil Cole is a Black architect whose outstanding work has put him at the pinnacle of his profession, especially when it comes to sports facilities. He is the founding principal of the Pendulum architecture firm, which is headquartered in the same neighborhood as the NLBM. Cole is a strong supporter of the Museum, so much so that he designed a new Negro Leagues Campus to replace the current undersized facility. At its heart will be the Buck O'Neil Education Center, which will be housed in the same building as the historic YMCA where the Negro Leagues were formed.

"The legacy of the Museum has impacted me in a tremendous way, and it is an honor to have a hand in its future with the design of the renovated Education Center," Cole explained. "In a world that often gets caught up in where you are from or how you might look, especially in an industry as competitive as sports architecture, what resonates is how you answer a simple question: Can you play? This was the question always posed by Rube Foster. He was the one who created a path for all of us to provide that answer."

Foster initially wanted his league to be entirely Black-run, but he accepted white owner J.L. Wilkinson of the Kansas City Monarchs because of the success of his franchise and Foster's high regard for

Wilkinson. In other words, he knew Wilkinson could "play."

During the boom years of the early 1920s, the Negro National League—under the iron-fisted leadership of Foster, ably assisted by the inventive Wilkinson—did remarkable business at the gate. In 1923, over 400,000 fans attended NNL games.

In the spring of 1920, C.I. Taylor's Indianapolis ABCs traveled to Birmingham to train for the inaugural season of the Negro National League. Oscar Charleston, considered by many the greatest player in the history of the Negro Leagues, was a young outfielder for the ABCs. Ben Taylor, C.I.'s brother, was also with the team. He was a .324 lifetime hitter (by existing known records) and the top first baseman of his era in Black baseball. Birmingham's Black baseball community, starved for baseball by a decade of piecemeal diamond offerings, grabbed hungrily at the morsels of information delivered by local media from the ABCs camp.

As the Indianapolis ABCs departed to begin the inaugural season of the Negro National League, talk of a new Negro league—one that would include a franchise in Birmingham—had captured the imagination of the city's Black districts. The rumors became reality, and in 1920 the Birmingham All-Stars (the name "Black Barons" still enjoyed popular acceptance and gradually superseded the new franchise's chosen nickname) began play in the Negro Southern League. Frank M. Perdue, the leading light (part owner and manager) of the Birmingham team, became president of the new league, and the city of Birmingham quickly garnered a reputation as the Black baseball capital of the American South.

Norman "Turkey" Stearnes, a Black legend of the 1920s and 1930s who is believed to have more career homers than Josh Gibson, first played in Rickwood Field in 1921 as a twenty-year-old rookie outfielder for the Black Barons' primary Negro Southern League rival, the Montgomery Grey Sox. The big-time atmosphere of Black baseball at Rickwood impressed Stearnes. "Memphis was a good baseball town, but Birmingham was the best in the South," Stearnes told a writer, years later, while reminiscing about the early days of the NSL. The Black Barons' gate appeal impressed Stearnes—"we'd draw 10-15,000." The solid fan support, along with access to Rickwood Field (one of the best ballparks in the country to be used as a home field by a Negro League team) resulted in Birmingham's elevation to big-league status in 1924, when the Black Barons entered the Negro National League.

The Black Barons brought talented players with them to the NNL. Mule Suttles, who is now credited with an all-time Negro Leagues record of 180 confirmed home runs in league games, hit 13 homers for Birmingham in 74 games in 1920—a staggering total for a player regularly batting at Rickwood, with its mammoth dimensions. "Spitballing Sam" Streeter and Harry "Fish" Salmon gave the Black Barons outstanding pitching. Saul Davis became a star infielder for a number of top NNL clubs.

Despite their talented players, fine facilities, and passionate fan support, the Black Barons struggled during their early days in the NNL. The distance from Birmingham to the other league cities forced them to spend even more time on the road than the typical barnstorming Negro League ballclub, and the strain showed in the Black Barons' record. The team also began to lose top players, such as Mule Suttles and Saul Davis, to better-financed Northern teams. In 1926, the Black Barons dropped out of the circuit for a year and returned to the Black minor leagues, back in the Negro Southern League.

While playing the Chattanooga Giants (later the Chattanooga Black Lookouts) on May 16, 1926, Birmingham got a look at a skinny pitcher named Leroy Paige, who was pitching his first professional baseball game. Already nicknamed "Satchel" (he was listed in most box scores of the period by his nickname rather than his given name), Paige defeated the Black Barons, 5-4. Apparently, Birmingham management was impressed by the hard-throwing youngster, because it gave him $275 a month to pitch for the Black Barons in 1927. This presented Satchel with an easy decision since he'd been earning $50 a month with Chattanooga.

Armed with their new phenom, the Birmingham Black Barons re-entered the Negro National League in 1927. Their team photo that year, taken in April at Rickwood, shows a very young Satchel Paige standing on the extreme left of the second row. Paige does not appear to have reached his full adult height of 6'3" in the photo, the first known photo of Satchel in a baseball uniform. He is a man barely out of boyhood, standing with veteran big-league ballplayers—men such as Streeter and Salmon. The image, by a photographer from Cloud Studio of Birmingham, captures Paige, yet to take the mound in a Negro major league game, at the beginning of a baseball odyssey.

Satchel Paige with the 1927 Birmingham Black Barons - earliest known photo of Paige in baseball uniform

Black Barons manager Ruben Jones appears to have held the young Paige out of the early going in the 1927 NNL season. Satchel's first known appearance in a big-league game came late in the first half of the NNL split season, on June 27 in St. Louis. Paige's apparent debut, although unknown to Negro League scholars prior to research done for the original edition of this book in 1995, was memorable. It was memorable not so much for how Paige entered as for how he exited.

Paige started for the Black Barons in the game against the St.

Louis Stars at Star Park. In the bottom of the second inning, with the score tied 1-1 and two away, Paige hit Stars catcher Mitchell Murray on the hand with a hard fastball. An enraged Murray charged the mound, brandishing his bat. From the grandstand, a fan bellowed to Satchel, "You have nothing to defend yourself with. Run, boy, run!" Paige took off for the safety of the Birmingham dugout but did not make it. Murray heaved his bat at Paige, striking the pitcher in the back just above the hip. A near-riot ensued, with fans taking the field, some carrying knives and blackjacks. Police officers had to restore order, and the game was called, bringing to a close Satchel Paige's first NNL start.

The Birmingham Reporter, in its report of the melee, made some interesting observations about Satchel Paige, including one that may help lay to rest lingering doubts about the true birth date of the pitcher. "It is to be remembered," noted *The Reporter*, "that Paige is a young fellow *nearly six feet, about 21 years old*, and throws the fastest and hardest ball in the circuit. On this occasion he was throwing hard, fast, and wild."

The article from *The Reporter* suggests that Paige had not attained his full growth in 1927, lending credence to the assertion that Satchel was no more than twenty-one years old, and not twenty-seven or some other higher age, as some have suggested. And the statement that Satchel threw "the fastest and hardest ball in the circuit" infers that Paige had pitched in previous contests for Birmingham in the 1927 NNL season, which means that Paige's debut appearance in the big leagues may still be undocumented.

To the baseball researcher, the most tantalizing bit of information in *The Reporter* article is the statement that Paige was "about 21 years old" in late June of 1927. Most reference books give Satchel's birth date as July 7, 1906. If this date is correct, Satchel would have turned twenty-one within two weeks of his appearance against the Stars in St. Louis. William J. Moore, the sports editor of *The Birmingham Reporter*, was an insider with the Black Barons, very familiar with the players, right down to their personal habits (he once complained in print that several Black Barons were spending too many nights out on the town). It is quite possible that Moore knew that Paige's twenty-first birthday was approaching when the article on the June 27 game (almost certainly written by Moore) appeared in *The Reporter*. Taken as a whole, the evidence in the article strongly supports the assertion that the accepted birth date for Satchel Paige—despite continuing contentions to the contrary—is accurate.

Little used during the first half of the split season, Satchel became a mainstay for the Black Barons in the second half. Using records that are available (which, of course, are incomplete and are revised regularly as more statistics are compiled through research), Paige is thought to have won at least seven games for Birmingham in 1927, against two losses. He was definitely a power pitcher: in 98 innings he struck out 93 batters, a truly remarkable ratio for the era.

By comparison, it is interesting to note that an outstanding power pitcher in the white major leagues during the 1920s, such as Hall of Famer Lefty Grove, usually struck out around two batters for each three innings pitched. Paige averaged close to a strikeout per inning. Satchel hurled three shutouts in '27, a total that would have ranked second in the American League that season—and Satchel had only about one-fourth as many starts as a typical white major league pitcher.

The Black Barons surged behind their newly discovered ace, winning the second-half championship of the Negro National League. Although Birmingham lost the league championship playoff to the Chicago American Giants, it had been the most successful season ever for the Black Barons in the NNL.

Paige enjoyed even more success in 1928, although the fortunes of the Black Barons declined. Satchel's known records for the campaign are impressive: an 11-4 won-loss record; 10 complete games; 121 strikeouts in 132 innings; a sparkling ERA of 2.32; only 7.7 hits allowed per 9 innings; and using modern rules (it wasn't an officially recognized statistic until 1969), he had four saves. Perhaps the most impressive stat on Paige's ledger for '28 is his base-on-balls total: only 25. Beyond this, he hit only three batters and uncorked only two wild pitches. All of this signifies terrific control as well as maturity beyond Satchel's twenty-two years.

The 1929 season stands out in Paige's baseball career for a number of reasons. Satchel set what might be the all-time Negro League strikeout record that season—at least 189 confirmed Ks in 186 innings. Even with the three-year research project commissioned by MLB in late 2020 to incorporate the stats of Negro League players into the history of the big leagues, we still don't have definitive records for the Negro Leagues, particularly in the 1920s. However, even with Paige's amazing strikeout prowess, his overall productivity for the Birmingham Black Barons dipped that year. His established record declined to 11-9, but his ERA was a respectable 3.68. It appears that Paige might well have been overworked. Since the Negro National League schedule usually ran about 80 games, Satchel was working at a rate that would have put him over 400 innings during a white major league season. As it was, he appeared in over a third of his team's games in '29.

Although his effectiveness varied throughout the year, Satchel Paige hit heights in 1929 that, in all probability, no Birmingham pitcher—regardless of race—has approached since. In the season opener at Rickwood Field on April 29, 1929, Paige struck out 17 Cuban Stars in winning a 6-2 decision. At the time, no white big leaguer had ever registered as many strikeouts in a single nine-inning game. Later in the season in Detroit, Satchel struck out 17 a second time in beating Bingo DeMoss' Stars, allowing only two hits. To close out his season of extremes, Satchel won both ends of a doubleheader at Rickwood against the Memphis Red Sox on the last day of the NNL campaign.

Paige began the 1930 season with the Baltimore Black Sox of the Negro American League. Whether this was done with the Black Barons' consent or Paige bolted from Birmingham for his own reasons is a matter of debate. If Satchel thought he was going to be the number-one starter in Baltimore, it didn't happen, and he was back pitching with the Black Barons by mid-season, where he won seven games in 12 appearances. Records also indicate he pitched two games for the Chicago American Giants in 1930. All of his team-hopping illustrates how difficult it is to compile definitive statistics. Regardless, his legend, burnished by his showmanship and barnstorming, remains intact even if his official stats are muddled.

Satchel left Birmingham for good in 1931, jumping to the Cleveland Cubs of the NNL before moving on to the mighty Pittsburgh Crawfords. In all, we believe he pitched for the following Negro League teams: Mobile Tigers (a semipro team when he was a teenager growing up in Mobile); Chattanooga Giants/Black Lookouts; Birmingham Black Barons; Baltimore Black Sox; Chicago American Giants; Cleveland Cubs; Pittsburgh Crawfords; Kansas City Monarchs; New York Black Yankees; Memphis Red Sox; Philadelphia Stars and many, many others while barnstorming. He finished his career in "white" baseball with the Cleveland Indians and St. Louis Browns ... and in 1965 at age fifty-nine, he started a major league game for the Kansas City Athletics, hurling three scoreless innings. Amazingly, he made the American League All-Star team in 1953 while playing for St. Louis at the age of forty-seven.

There will never be a player like Satchel Paige again.

His official record while pitching in a Black Barons uniform was 36-17—although some records indicate he might have won as many as 44 games. But even at 36-17, that's a sparkling winning percentage of .679.

When Paige left the Black Barons in '31, it was just before the Negro National League folded. The twin blows of the loss of Rube Foster (who died in 1930 after being incapacitated for four years by mental illness) and the crash of the American economy were more than the NNL could take. The Birmingham Black Barons, so successful a few short years earlier, were out of business. It would be six long, hot Birmingham summers before Black baseball returned to Rickwood.

CHAPTER 8

THE BABE OF THE BUSH

Prior to 2004, any baseball fan worthy of the title "fan" believed in his heart of hearts that there was a curse on the Boston Red Sox. The Sox hadn't won a Series in modern memory. Sure, they'd won lots of them—five to be exact—but all of those championships had been decided before the Armistice ended The War to End All Wars. Four years into a new millennium, Yankees fans chanted at Red Sox players, "Nineteen-eighteen!" That was the year the last World Series banner had been hung at Fenway Park.

Some blamed the curse on the sale of Babe Ruth to the New York Yankees on January 5, 1920. After all, that happened just after Harry Frazee's Sox had last won the world championship. Others believe that the evil spell predated the Bambino's career and was responsible for the tragic injury that robbed immortal Boston pitcher Smoky Joe Wood of the lightning in his right arm. For whatever reason, it was said misfortune stalked the residents of Fenway Park. The mental collapse of Jimmy Piersall and the horrific beaning of Tony Conigliaro are two prominent examples of the baseball miseries that had befallen Massachusetts.

But in 2004, Fenway Futility ended. The Red Sox won it all. That was followed by three more crowns in the next decade and a half. The curse had been broken decisively and (for the long-suffering fans of New England) joyfully.

Perhaps it was a supernatural force that kept Red Sox outfielder Elliot Bigelow from the baseball immortality he seemed destined to achieve. The name does not conjure up images of titanic home runs, or slashing line drives, or of pennants won by talent and grit, does it? The name inspires only a quizzical look and the inevitable question: *Who*?

A few obsessed baseball researchers know who Elliot Bigelow was, and in years past some (really) older residents of Birmingham and Chattanooga could still remember the Jazz Age days when "Sandy" Bigelow or "Babe" Bigelow or "Gilly" Bigelow (Southern sportswriters liked to hang nicknames on ballplayers, especially ones with nerdy names like Elliot) was the greatest player in a fine minor league. Bigelow, playing for the Chattanooga Lookouts and Birmingham Barons in the mid- to late 1920s, posted a .359 lifetime batting average, making him, according to the Society for American Baseball Research (SABR), the all-time batting champion of the Southern Association.

Earlier in his career, the 5'11", 185 lb. outfielder had slogged through *five* years in the Florida State League, although he provided a dominant season in 1922, leading the circuit in batting (a .343 average), triples, doubles, and hits. When he was between the lines of a ballfield he excelled. However, the world beyond the ballpark conspired against Elliot Bigelow. He remained a captive of the bushes until he emerged at Fenway at age thirty-one, a Roy Hobbsian figure—past his prime but still showing the flashes of brilliance that made him the idol of Birmingham's youth.

He had arrived in Birmingham in 1927. Rick Woodward had taken notice of Bigelow's outstanding play in Chattanooga (.349 average, 111 RBIs, 66 extra-base hits in 1925; .370 average, 118 RBI and a whopping 86 extra-base hits in 1926), and, as part of the Barons owner's plan to buy a pennant, Woodward purchased the best-hitting outfielder in the South as the keystone of his baseball team. Woodward had already obtained the services of the best baseball manager in the minor leagues, veteran Johnny Dobbs. He was hired by the Barons after the horrendous 1924 season (an all-time Birmingham record 98 losses), making the Magic City one of the last stops in a storied career in which he managed in the Southern Association for twenty-five years, winning six pennants. This was in addition to the newly hired talent that already featured speedy infielder Stuffy Stewart, who had cups of coffee with the Cardinals and Dodgers and wound up his career with an all-time Southern

Association record 371 stolen bases. The city of Birmingham was anticipating pennant contention for the first time in over a decade.

Rickwood Field is a pitcher's park. In its fifty-one seasons as a home in the Southern Association, only four league batting champions called Rickwood home. Further, only four winners of the home-run crown played for the Barons, and only three runs-scored leaders played in Birmingham. In two stunning seasons, Elliot Bigelow led the Southern Association in each of these offensive categories.

The 1927 season was perhaps Bigelow's greatest. He set a Birmingham record by driving in 143 runs to lead the Southern Association. He also led the league with 137 runs scored. Bigelow clubbed 20 homers, the second-highest total ever for a Birmingham Baron and a mark that would not be exceeded by anyone until the fences at Rickwood were moved closer to home plate in 1941. With a batting average of .359, he just missed notching a Triple Crown. His play sparked the Barons to a second-place finish, their best in eleven years.

In 1928, the Barons returned to the promised land after wandering in the wilderness for fourteen years. Behind Elliot Bigelow's all-time Barons record .395 average (and 123 RBIs despite missing three weeks with an injury), Johnny Dobbs won his fifth pennant in the Southern Association—and his first in the Magic City. The same Barons franchise that set an all-time record for losses four years earlier set an all-time record for wins—99 against only 54 losses—in bringing Rick Woodward his third flag as owner.

The Barons won with the bat in 1928. No other Southern Association team ever hit like Johnny Dobbs' Barons. As a team, Birmingham hit for an astonishing .331 average. Thirteen players hit .300 or over, adding to the total of league records set by Woodward's sluggers. Other all-time records set by the '28 Barons include most hits and most triples.

The majors finally gave Elliot Bigelow a chance in 1929. He opened the season with the Red Sox as an outfielder, but his playing time was limited. He played only 58 games in the field, although he pinch-hit in 42 more. He proved to be a solid hitter at the major league level, batting .284 in the tough role of spot player and pinch-hitter. After the '29 season, though, Bigelow was sent back to the minors. The brass at Fenway felt his throwing arm was weak, but Bigelow's age probably doomed his one shot at the big time. By the end of the 1932 season, he was out of baseball for good.

Elliot Bigelow returned to his native Florida after his playing days were through. He loved fishing as much as he had loved baseball, and he hoped to live out his days as a commercial fisherman on the Gulf near Tampa, where the tropical sun could sear away the memories of diamond disappointment forever.

But it was not to be. The Fenway Curse, it seems, could always find its prey.

In August 1933, as Rick Woodward's team struggled through a miserable summer, a very old young man died in Florida, a victim of cerebral meningitis. Elliot Bigelow was thirty-five, young for a man, old for a ballplayer, and ancient for a phenom.

CHAPTER 9
SUMMER AND SMOKE

The Roaring Twenties exited a happy but anxious Birmingham. The 1929 Barons had taken a second straight Southern Association championship, clinching the title a little over a month before Wall Street crashed and burned. The smoke from the wreckage of America's financial infrastructure hovered over industrial Birmingham as a critical decade in the fortunes of Birmingham—and Rick Woodward—began.

The '20s had been good for the city. Growth was strong. The steel industry was solid. Civic pride was justifiably high. The Jazz Age had also been kind to Rick Woodward, who used some of the profits from his booming ironworks to renovate Rickwood Field. The new construction marked the first extensive changes to the structure since the ballpark was built in 1910.

In 1924, the roof had been extended over the concrete bleachers along the first-base line. New steel bleachers were added down the left-field line. Paul Wright and Company, an engineering firm, did the design work for the project.

The third-base-side concrete bleachers were covered in 1927, with the architectural firm Denham, VanKeuren, and Denham handling the design. As in the previous expansion, new box seats were added to the newly roofed areas of Rickwood.

A final expansion in 1928 gave Rickwood the form that survives to the present day. Paul Wright and Company, back on the job for Woodward, designed the now-familiar covered grandstand that

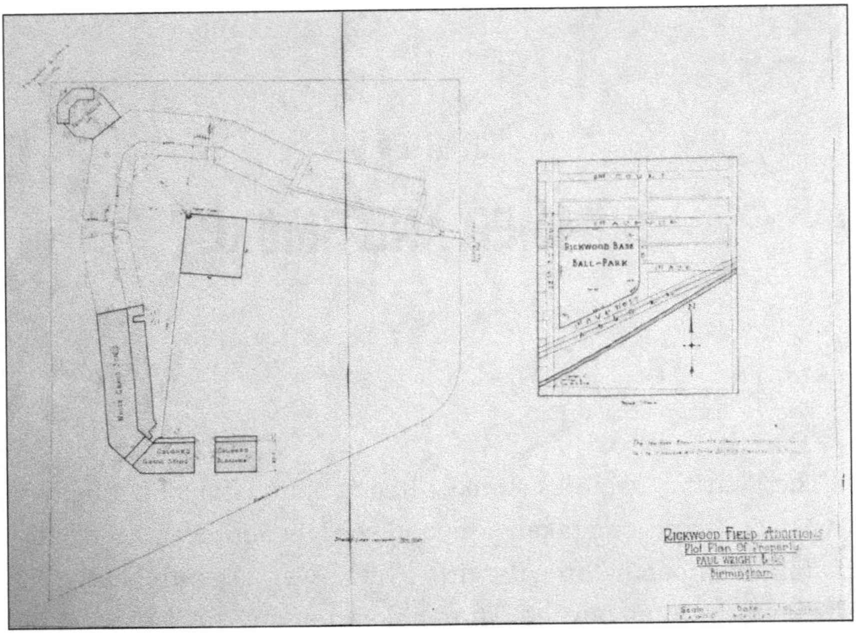

Architectural Drawings for the Rickwood Field Expansion and Remodeling, 1928

Aerial View of Rickwood after the 1928 expansion and remodeling

runs down the right-field line before curving around the foul pole and extending along the outfield fence. Next to this grandstand, exposed to the sun in the deep outfield, sat the new "Negro bleachers," the only section of seats ever constructed at Rickwood that no longer exist, as those bleachers were demolished years later.

The 1928 expansion also gave Rickwood its distinctive entry arcade. The arcade is a Spanish Mission-style structure, an odd choice for ballpark architecture, but a selection that makes sense given the taste of Birmingham (and Rick Woodward) in 1928. Mission-style houses, connected in the public mind to the glamour of movie stars in Southern California, were all the rage in the American South in the 1920s. A Birmingham suburban development of the time, called (naturally) "Hollywood," featured a number of "Southern California bungalows," many of which still stand. A drive down Homewood's Hollywood Boulevard affords the opportunity to see a number of these houses today. Rick Woodward himself built a huge mansion atop Red Mountain in the '20s that aped a noted residence in Pasadena, California. The Woodward House, perhaps the most expensive private residence ever constructed in Alabama, shares the stucco and clay-tile roof of the original entryway at Rickwood.

The ballpark's entry arcade consists of a colonnaded one-story porch connected to a two-story structure. The ground floor of the arcade served as the gate for Rickwood Field, while the second story housed the Barons offices. Between the arcade and the grandstand is a breezeway. Since the grandstand at Rickwood is oriented to the field (laid out by Connie Mack according to the position of the sun), while the arcade is square with the street corner, the arcade is *not* parallel to the breezeway. From the air, this gives an odd, bent look to the entrance of Rickwood.

Today you'd just refer to it as quirky. But quirky can be endearing in ballpark design.

The '28 entry arcade replaced an earlier structure that had been constructed along with the grandstand in 1910. The original entry to Rickwood was separate from the ballpark, but much closer to the grandstand than the 1928 arcade. The 1910 gate appears to have

The massive hand-operated scoreboard installed at Rickwood in 1928

stood on the site of the present breezeway.

Two other notable additions to Rickwood were made during the 1928 expansion. The concrete wall, replacing the original wooden fence (which had been heavily damaged by a tornado in March of 1921—work crews hurriedly replaced the damage before Opening Day), was installed. And against the new concrete wall in deep left center field, a magnificent, forty-foot-tall hand-operated scoreboard took its place in Rickwood and in Birmingham's baseball memory.

The original Rickwood scoreboard still evokes powerful emotions in those who remember it. To the batters at the time, already humbled by the distant reaches of the outfield walls, the height of the board must have seemed like a stop sign. For pitchers who saw a hanging curve ball batted down to a mere double by the scoreboard, it must have seemed like a sign of forgiveness. Like the present manual scoreboard at Fenway Park, it featured the scores of other games in progress as well as the contest being played at Rickwood. A special feature of the Rickwood board was that it listed the scores of American League and National League games along with the Southern Association matchups. To young fans in the bleachers at Rickwood, the far-off big leagues seemed closer when the up-to-the-minute update in the Giants-Dodgers score appeared on the board, dropped into position by a much-envied teenager inside the scoreboard.

View of the 1928 entry arcade at Rickwood, showing the "Hollywood" influence on the architecture

If there had been any doubt about Rickwood's status as the finest ballpark in the Southern Association, the flurry of construction in the 1920s shut down all argument. Rickwood Field enjoyed universal recognition as a fine playground ... and as a playground for fine teams.

In three of the first four seasons that the Barons played at the "new" Rickwood Field (1928, 1929 and 1931), Birmingham captured the Southern Association pennant. The 1927 club, which won over 90 games in finishing second, and the 1930 Barons, who finished third, were also solid, contending clubs. With a bit of luck, they could have been league champs five straight times. The Barons teams of this era really hit the ball, as between 1926 and 1931, Birmingham's *team* batting average never dipped below .297. In fact, the six highest team batting averages in Barons history are these six years. Batsmen led by slugger Elliot Bigelow, powerful and popular catcher Clarence Everett "Yam" Yaryan, speedy Stuffy Stewart, and steady Art "Butch" Weis (who smacked 20 homers in 1931) paced those Rickwood powerhouses.

Fine pitchers, though often overshadowed by the most potent offense in loop history, worked for Birmingham in the late '20s and early '30s. Lefty Eddie Wells recorded a remarkable 38-8 mark over the 1927-28 seasons. His 13-1 mark in '27 set an all-time winning percentage record for the Barons, topping "General" Alvin

Crowder's 17-4 ledger from 1925. Crowder, by the way, went on to win 167 games in the majors against only 115 losses, an impressive .592 winning percentage—especially when you consider his career ERA was 4.12. Bob Hasty twice won 20 games for Birmingham, and Willie Ludolph, "Little Jimmy" Walkup, and Ray Caldwell all topped the 20-win mark once.

Dobbs exhibited skill and experience during his time as manager in the Magic City, as evidenced by his championships in '28 and '29. He came to town as a living legend, and he's generally acknowledged as the greatest manager in Southern Association history. When Dobbs defected to the hated Atlanta Crackers in 1930, Clyde Milan, a fine big-league outfielder in the 1910s (and, like Dobbs, a Tennessee native) took over. Milan and the '31 Barons seized the fifth flag for Rick Woodward, and Birmingham appeared to have built an impregnable dynasty.

But even as the '31 championship was celebrated, the Great Depression sapped the industrial strength from the city. Meanwhile, one of the brashest pitchers in history had made his way from Arkansas to Texas, and he was gunning for the Barons in the biggest baseball showdown ever in Alabama.

CHAPTER 10

DIZZY AND RAY

"Wire me 150 words every day on Dizzy Dean," wrote Zipp Newman, sports editor of *The Birmingham News,* to a sportswriter friend who covered the Houston Buffaloes, champions of the Texas League. "What does he do to pass time? What does he eat? Let's have all the dope. He's started a stampede here for tickets. His name has already become a household word. From what you hear, you would think he's the whole Houston ballclub. The common impression around town is, 'What do you think Dizzy will do in the series?' And the answer is pack Rickwood Field as it has never been packed before."

Jay Hanna Dean was a dirt-poor sharecropper's son from Lucas, Arkansas. His education topped out at the second grade. He emerged from the cotton fields of western Arkansas a somewhat mysterious figure whose true given name was not known for sure for decades. In a similar fashion to his great friend Satchel Paige's evasive answers about his age, Dean often gave different responses about his given name; sometimes giving the (apparently) accurate "Jay Hanna Dean" and sometimes claiming the (allegedly) inaccurate "Jerome Herman Dean."

Dizzy was twenty-one years old in the summer of 1931. He had the best fastball and the biggest ego in baseball. Everything about Dean was oversized. He was big, he talked big, he played big, he even *lived* big. He already had a taste of the big leagues, as the previous September he'd made a start for the St. Louis Cardinals ... and pitched a complete game without surrendering an earned run! And in September of 1931, as his Buffs headed to Birmingham to tangle with the Southern Association champion Birmingham Barons in the Dixie Series, Dean loomed as the biggest challenge the Barons would ever face at Rickwood Field.

Dizzy Dean and Ray Caldwell before the First Game of the Dixie Series at Rickwood, September 16, 1931

Still the property of the Cards, he had won 26 games against 10 losses for the Buffs in '31, striking out 303 batters in 304 innings. Using modern-day calculations, his ERA was a paltry 1.57. Scouts said the young pitcher was faster than Walter Johnson in his prime.

Behind Dean and future Hall of Fame outfielder Joe "Ducky" Medwick, Houston compiled an eye-opening record of 108-45 that year. The Buffs set a new Texas League attendance record, drawing 230,000 fans, many of whom came to see if Dizzy Dean could back up his frequent boasts. "Tain't braggin' if you kin really do it!" was Dean's credo, and Dizzy tended to back up his words with action.

With the Texas circuit conquered, Dizzy turned his attention to Birmingham. Exclaimed the righthander, "If I don't beat them Barons, I'll join the House of David and grow a beard and never, never shave it off. It would hide my shame. I may pitch left-handed against them. That way they'd have a chance."

Birmingham was outraged. Didn't Dean know that the Barons had won the Southern Association pennant by 10½ games? The city, and the prestigious Southern Association, had been insulted. Now the Barons had to win. The sentiment around the Magic City was that Mr. Dean had to be taught a lesson in humility.

Dean referred to Birmingham manager Clyde Milan as "Deerfoot," an old nickname Milan picked up after stealing 88 bases for the 1912 Washington Senators. Unfortunately, Milan did not have a young phenom to send up against the mighty Buffs starter. In fact, he did not even name Bob Hasty, the ace of his experienced staff, or hot Jimmy Walkup, who had posted a 20-5 record in '31, to start the opening game of the Dixie Series against Dean. Instead, perhaps conceding the first game to the Buffs, Milan put the ball in the hands of forty-three-year-old Ray Caldwell.

Caldwell had once been a major leaguer, and a good one. Before Dizzy Dean was born, Ray "Slim" Caldwell was winning games for the New York Yankees and gaining recognition as "the next Chief Bender." In 1920, Caldwell won 20 games for the World Series champion Cleveland Indians. But by 1922, Ray Caldwell was gone from the big leagues, never to return.

Ray Caldwell drank. In a game known for its prodigious drinkers, Caldwell was the League Drunk. Tris Speaker, Caldwell's manager in Cleveland, actually inserted a clause in Ray's contract that *required* the pitcher to get drunk after every start. Speaker hoped that if Caldwell got drunk immediately after his turn in the rotation, he might be sober enough to pitch again in four days. Ray couldn't stay on the wagon, however, and he fell into the netherworld of the bush leagues, supporting himself with his eroding talents, hanging on for dear life to the raised stitches of the white ball.

Ray had found a decent life in Birmingham, especially for a has-been busher. He had married a local girl, his third try at marriage. He had lost two previous wives to the bottle and to baseball. The Barons were a good minor league organization, with great fan and community support. Ray felt important in Birmingham as a Baron, as it was a lot like being a New York Yankee or Cleveland Indian again. The neighborhood kids looked up to him, and prominent men in town liked to cozy up to team members. But to Ray Caldwell, the most important thing about being a Baron was getting the ball in his hand every four days. He loved the game and had sacrificed everything for the chance, at forty-three, to still be playing it.

By game time on September 16, Birmingham had reached the boiling point. Rickwood Field, which had never held more than 15,000 fans, was invaded by a crowd of 20,074—although for decades after, it was impossible to find any local fan of a certain age who did not claim to have witnessed this contest. It was the largest crowd ever to attend a sporting event in Alabama to that time.

Cars overflowed the Rickwood lot and lined 12th Street for

blocks—indicative of the limited parking capacity that would haunt team owners throughout the century as the automobile replaced the trolley as the preferred means of getting to games. Fans elbowed and jostled into the standing-room areas and swarmed onto the field along the baselines and in the deeper reaches of the outfield. On this day, the players of both teams appreciated the deep fences of the Birmingham ballpark. The "Negro bleachers" in right field overflowed as well, and fans there included a gangly kid named Lorenzo Davis attending his first professional game ... full of his own dreams of stardom that would play out on that very playing field eleven years in the future after he started going by his nickname "Piper."

Kids paraded up and down the aisle through the grandstand holding up chalkboards with handwritten messages from businesses attempting to communicate with their managers who were playing hooky from work to see the mighty Dean.

The hometown fans spotted the object of their ire as he took his warm-up tosses before the game. Boos rained down upon the relaxed figure of Dizzy Dean, who turned and retorted, "It'll be a breeze, like taking candy from a baby," to his hecklers. Soon, the Barons took the field amid a tumultuous roar, and Ray Caldwell eased slowly to the mound.

Game one of the best-of-seven series didn't start well for Caldwell and the Barons. Two of Houston's first three batters singled, and Medwick, the Texas League's leading home run hitter, pounded a long drive to deep left center field. In most parks the liner would have been a homer for sure, but it stayed in Rickwood, and, with help from obliging fans on the playing field who parted so he could make the catch, center fielder Woody Abernathy made a stumbling, over-the-shoulder grab of Medwick's rocket.

Through the first six innings, Caldwell stayed in trouble. Houston had base runners in every frame, while Dean had faced the minimum 18 Barons over the same stretch. Only two Birmingham players had reached base—one on a walk and the other on a weak single—and both had been erased by double plays. Caldwell gave up seven hits before the seventh inning, but he kept working the corners of the plate, kept nibbling away at the confident Houston batters. Not once in the entire game did Ray run the count full against a Buff.

In the seventh inning, Caldwell recorded his first strikeout of the game. The old man, to the surprise and consternation of Houston, was getting stronger as the contest wore on, just like he used to when he threw smoke for the Yankees. He struck out two Buffs in the Houston eighth, and now Birmingham came up in the bottom of the inning, against Dizzy Dean, who had allowed only two hits all day.

Diz quickly got two outs. He was one strike away from being out of the inning when rookie catcher Zach Taylor singled to right field. The next batter due up was Ray Caldwell.

In the eighth inning of a scoreless game, Clyde Milan knew that baseball logic called for the removal of his ancient pitcher for a pinch-hitter. Caldwell couldn't last much longer anyway, and this could very well be the Barons' only chance to get to Dizzy. But Clyde Milan knew Ray Caldwell. He had hit against a young Ray Caldwell twenty years earlier, and he had managed an old Ray Caldwell for the previous two seasons. What Clyde Milan knew—something no one else could know—kept the ball, and the game, in the leathery hands of the Barons' forty-three-year-old hurler.

As Caldwell approached the plate, the 20,074 fans, all on their feet (and most on their tiptoes), began to chant: "Hoo-RAY, Hoo-RAY!" The old pitcher, who had known so much of the downside of baseball, must have savored the moment. Then he stepped in against the pitcher young enough to be his son, and cocked his bat.

The fastball said to be faster than Johnson's raced for the plate. Ray Caldwell, who had faced Walter Johnson, brought his bat around to meet it. Once Ray, a fine hitter, might have been able to send a screaming line drive into the gap. Now, though, with his bones creaking, his best effort resulted in a weak grounder.

But it was enough. The grounder had eyes and found its way through the infield. Taylor advanced to third and Billy Bancroft, a local hero due to his football playing days at Birmingham's Howard College, stood in against Dizzy Dean.

Dean threw a fastball. Bancroft, way behind the pitch, swung for a strike. The second pitch, even faster, went by Bancroft without a challenge for strike two. Years later, Bancroft would still recall, with a touch of awe, the velocity of that throw.

Bancroft braced for a blazing strike three. But Diz proceeded to do the strangest thing.

Dean threw a curve.

Billy Bancroft jumped on the gift from the baseball gods. The ball jumped off his bat and over third base, cleanly inside the left-field line. The ball bounced into the crowd for a ground rule double.

Cheering was reported in every small town within twenty-five miles of Birmingham as radio listeners heard that Taylor had crossed the plate with the game's first and only run.

Ray Caldwell returned to the mound for the top of the ninth. The befuddled Buffs were no match for the rejuvenated hurler, as he set them down one-two-three, recording two more strikeouts.

The Birmingham Barons claimed a 1-0 win in game one. The happy partisans lifted the aging pitcher onto their shoulders and carried him off the Rickwood Field turf. And for the first time in his professional career, Dizzy Dean had failed to strike out a single batter.

There would be other games in the series, of course. Houston bounced back to take game two in Birmingham, 3-0. Licensed locomotive engineer Rick Woodward gleefully guided the train carrying the players and the forty-five-member Police Band out of Birmingham's Terminal Station, bound for Houston to do battle in the next three games. In front of their home fans, the Buffs blanked the Barons in games three and four, with Dean picking up the shutout to push Birmingham to the brink of elimination.

Coming off three straight shutouts, the Barons' bats bounced back enough to post a 3-1 win in game five, sending the series back to Alabama. The bats really came to life in game six at Rickwood, as the Barons had 23 hits on their way to a 14-10 win, forcing a seventh game in the series.

The modern playoff format of 2-3-2 wasn't in effect, so the deciding game wasn't in Birmingham. Game seven was back on the south side of Houston on September 25. The Barons' starter was Bob Hasty. He faced Dizzy Dean, who had just been informed that he was heading to St. Louis after the game to finish off the big-league season with the Buffs' parent team. After striking out five of the first six Barons he faced, Dean faltered and Birmingham took a 3-2 lead into the ninth. There they pushed three more runners across the plate, although two of them were unearned. The Buffs weren't done, as they rallied to score a run in the bottom of the ninth with one out. With the two most potent bats due up for Houston (Medwick and Homer Peel, who amassed 42 extra-base hits that season), manager Milan pulled Hasty, electing to bring in Caldwell to put out the fire.

After a tense showdown with Medwick resulted in a strikeout, Caldwell coaxed a ground ball out of Peel, and the visitors completed the shocking upset of the heavily favored Buffs with a 6-3 victory in the deciding game. Caldwell had provided bookends for this seminal series.

The joyous Barons returned to a hero's welcome in Birmingham, leaving the thunderstruck Buffs and a humbled Houston in their wake. In a publication called *The Pecan Park Eagle,* baseball historian Bill McCurdy (who passed away in 2019) penned an insightful essay eighty years after this series about how affected his maternal grandfather was by the Houston Buffs' loss in '31: "(t)he man we all called "Papa" was very unhappy with the Buffs loss, but he also liked to later use this story as an example of how we can never take anything for granted in life. The Buffs may have won this Series in their own minds in advance, but they didn't then go out and win it on the field, according to Papa. These also were the early years of the Great Depression, when some even harder lessons about taking things for granted were raining down on Papa and a lot of other folks caught up in the great economic and agricultural dust storm

... The lesson for me came down to this statement by Papa: "Don't count your chickens before they hatch, even if you have Dizzy Dean sitting on the eggs."

History shows that Birmingham won the 1931 Dixie Series over the overconfident Buffs four games to three, but it is the first game of the series that became a legend. It is the game that is remembered in Birmingham, even today. The game is the touchstone of Birmingham's baseball experience, forever etched into the city's collective memory.

In 1950, the Birmingham Barons celebrated the 40th anniversary of Rickwood Field by inviting several baseball stars of the past to appear in a pre-game ceremony of honors. The dignitaries included baseball Hall of Famers, Southern Association officials, and local celebrities. But the loudest ovation of the evening—a thunderous salute that stopped the proceedings—went to a sixty-two-year-old American Legion Post manager from New Jersey named Ray Caldwell, who by one afternoon's heroics erased a lifetime of frustration to become the most beloved figure in Birmingham Barons history.

CHAPTER 11
THE CHILL RAINS COME

The long summer of Rick Woodward's life came to a close on a winter day in 1938.

Although he would live another dozen years, the sixty-one-year-old sportsman reluctantly turned over his beloved baseball team and every bit as beloved ballpark to Birmingham businessman Ed Norton on February 7, 1938. Norton, who made his money in the automobile business, not in the sewers of New York like the Art Carney character that shared his name, paid $175,000 for Woodward's baseball legacy. It was a steal, as Woodward had invested over half a million dollars in Rickwood Field alone during his twenty-eight years of ownership.

Woodward had no choice but to sell his favorite toy. He needed the cash. In 1936, the Woodward Iron Company had been forced into bankruptcy reorganization. The Depression had been devastating for the iron-and-steel industry, and Woodward's business had taken a number of hard blows. Many of the problems could be traced to poor decisions made by executives at Woodward Iron as the crisis developed in the late 1920s. By the time Rick cleaned house with a round of firings (including the removal of the president of Woodward Iron) in 1932, the damage had been done.

In retrospect, Woodward may have wished that he had seized a golden opportunity presented to him in 1930. Both the Republic Steel Corporation and Bethlehem Steel offered Rick $30 million for his family business. Woodward held out for $35 million, and the deal was undone. A chance at amassing a huge fortune—one greater than any other "baron" on the Birmingham business scene—disappeared due to the omnipresent myopic vision of Depression-era

Elderly Rick Woodward

industrialists. The steel industry had always come back, bigger and better than ever, from past panics and recessions. The great industrialists never doubted that American industry would keep right on growing, right on booming, for decades to come. Rick Woodward held onto the company that had made him rich.

Adding to his other financial woes, Woodward began a war with the merciless combatants of the Internal Revenue Service. Not long after he sold the Barons and Rickwood Field, Woodward found himself slapped with a bill for $55,000 in back taxes. Despite Woodward's fervent protests, the IRS collected the stated amount, leaving the once-flamboyant multimillionaire quite cash-poor as the 1940s began. World War II and the resulting demand for iron and steel helped restore his wealth, but Rick never again lived in the grand style that had been his custom earlier in the century when he drove Birmingham's first automobile into town when coming home from college.

He had grown old—almost overnight, it seemed to the Birmingham sports fans who had grown up reading regular accounts of his exploits in the local papers. Rick rarely ventured into the public eye as the midpoint of the 20th century approached. He spent most of his days behind the walls of his great estate on Red Mountain, far from the ballpark in which he had invested the passion of his youthful love for baseball. He seemed to have divorced himself from his old obsessions. He no longer attended games at Rickwood.

But the old fires still burned inside Rick. The flame that had been kindled inside a sixteen-year-old boy at Sewanee in the last decade of the 19th century still smoldered inside the wealthy seventy-year-old industrialist of the Cold War era. Even though he avoided the ballpark, Woodward enjoyed reminiscing about the grand old times, and he secretly wished that his old friends in baseball would seek him out. On occasion, he complained that the only people in baseball who even gave him the courtesy of a Christmas card were Bill McGilvray—who had but two plate appearances in the big leagues but topped 2,500 for Rick's Barons in the 1910s—and Stuffy Stewart, his reliable second baseman in the 1920s.

As summer turned into fall in 1950, Woodward spent his time at the country club he had built near his family's ironworks, silently watching the young golfers. The celebration of the fortieth anniversary of Rickwood Field's opening came and went. Not feeling well, Woodward sent his oldest son Joe in his stead to the festivities. In September, the Barons finished their season, placing second in the Southern Association, and Rick Woodward turned seventy-four, the same age that Joseph Hersey Woodward had been when he died.

October brought the World Series and a predictable triumph for the DiMaggio-led Yankees. And then came November, and suddenly there was no baseball at all. Rick still reported to the Woodward Country Club daily, to watch the young at their games, but by late in the month the weather had turned cold, and there were no more games to be played.

On November 23, 1950, the first snowfall of the year fell on Birmingham. As an early winter settled on the city, high atop Red Mountain, Rick Woodward, a lover of the summer, died.

CHAPTER 12

NIGHTTIME BASEBALL

The Depression years were bad for the Barons, but the World War II years were worse. While annual attendance at Rickwood had not dipped below 125,000 between 1919 and 1931, attendance did not exceed 78,000 from 1932 to 1936. Jim Burt, the Barons general manager and Rick Woodward's son-in-law, had towering light standards installed in 1936, and the novelty of night baseball spurred the gate count to nearly 200,000, the best since 1929. That success, however, was short-lived. In 1940, the Barons drew only 74,000 fans, and during the war, Birmingham managed to exceed 100,000 fans on just one occasion.

Iconic light standards at Rickwood at time of installation, 1936

Hard times hurt the Barons at the gate, but poor performances hurt them more. From 1932 to 1949, Birmingham finished no better than third place in the Southern Association. Having once again grown accustomed to winners, Birmingham fans did not take to the mediocre teams put on the field by the Barons' new ownership. Ed Norton kept the team for only two poor seasons, then sold it to the Cincinnati Reds, who kept the franchise through most of World War II. With many Birmingham industries idle, a dollar was hard to come by in the once Magic City, and few wanted to waste a cent on a second-division ball club run by absentee owners.

In an effort to spur attendance, the Reds had the Rickwood fences moved closer to home for the first time in 1941, constructing a wooden fence running inside the concrete wall that had imprisoned so many long fly balls. The move was designed to produce crowd-pleasing home runs—and it did. Baron Al Mele hit 17 homers for the season to top Dutch Bernsen's long-standing record. The Barons drew a bit better in their slightly cozier park, and the style of baseball played at Rickwood began to more closely resemble the power-hitting game popular in the big leagues since the early '20s, when the phenomenon of Babe Ruth came along.

In the meantime, a new Black Barons franchise emerged in 1937, playing in the newly formed Negro American League. The economic footing for a Black team in Birmingham, particularly considering the difficulty of the white Barons in drawing fans, must have been particularly fragile, but the Birmingham Black Barons beat the odds.

Birmingham baseball had not fully recovered from the Depression when World War II arrived, complete with new, unprecedented difficulties. Baseball's talent pool was drained to dirt-dry. The 1944 Barons program indicated that not one of the roster players held a draft status of 1-A. The inclusion of a player's draft status in the program underscored the tenuous grasp a team had on a ballplayer during wartime.

The Black Barons fared slightly better at keeping their marquee players in Birmingham. Stars Lorenzo "Piper" Davis, Artie Wilson,

Lorenzo "Piper" Davis, star player on multiple Birmingham Black Baron NAL pennant-winning teams

Lester Lockett, and Ted "Double Duty" Radcliffe all played at Rickwood during the war. In fact, the war years were glory years for Birmingham's Negro American League entry, with the Black Barons winning back-to-back NAL pennants in 1943 and 1944. After both seasons, the Black Barons faced the powerful Homestead Grays of the Negro National League in the Negro League World Series.

The Negro World Series never attained the popularity of the great Negro League East-West All-Star Games generally held at Comiskey Park in Chicago.

The World Series of the Negro Leagues theoretically decided the championship of Black baseball in America. The two league champions often played the Series by barnstorming around the country for publicity, sometimes even playing exhibitions in the middle of the championship contests. The Series soon lost credibility with the fans.

Another factor that diminished the importance of the Series was the often-mercurial nature of the Negro Leagues, or more precisely, the players themselves. Players sometimes changed teams several times in a season, attracted by better pay or conditions or publicity, all of which tended to undermine fan loyalty to one team. It was often easier to follow the career of one hero such as a Josh Gibson or Satchel Paige than the team they were playing for, a practice that fed the popularity of the All-Star contests showcasing the individual stars. The Series was important to the Black Barons, but winning the league championship reportedly held more value in the players' eyes.

The Black Barons came within an eyelash of winning the Negro Series in 1943, taking the loaded Grays (which split their home games between Pittsburgh and Washington each season) to seven games before falling short. The memorable sixth game of the series featured a pitchers' duel won by Birmingham's John Markham, 1-0. "Father of the Blues" W.C. Handy pulled for the Black Barons from a Rickwood box.

In the 1944 Series, again against the Grays, the opener drew 12,449 war-weary fans to Rickwood looking for a taste of victory, but the Black Barons, playing without three players (including star switch-hitting catcher Lloyd "Pepper" Bassett) who had been injured in a car wreck one week earlier, went down with barely a whimper, swept in four games.

As the war reached its conclusion, Birmingham outwardly appeared little different than it had four years earlier. The war had spurred the iron and steel industries, releasing the shackles of Depression that had tortured Birmingham as cruelly as any city in the nation, and giving birth to a new spirit of optimism. The future looked promising once again, perhaps as promising as it had in 1910, when Birmingham was the fastest-growing metropolis in the land.

But the war had changed Birmingham, just as America had changed. Black soldiers, returning home to the country for whom they had risked their lives, brought more home than the medals on their chests. They brought a raised expectation of fair and equal treatment as American citizens. But in Birmingham, as in the rest of America, the world was still have and have-not, the front door and the back, and baseball's color line was still solidly intact.

CHAPTER 13

THE GLENNON YEARS

On March 10, 1944, Warren Giles, general manager of the Cincinnati Reds of the National League, met with a gentleman of middle years from Birmingham. G.J. (Gus) Jebeles had retired from the hotel business a year earlier, but he had one final deal he wished to close, and so he journeyed north to Cincy.

Thirty-nine years earlier, Gus Jebeles had been Konstantenous John Jebeles, seventeen years old and recently arrived in Birmingham from his native Greece. Although his family had lived in Birmingham for several years in the 1890s, the Jebeles clan had returned to Greece in 1897. But young Konstantenous loved America and returned to Birmingham as soon as he was deemed a man by his family. Back in Alabama, Jebeles attended a Barons game at the old Slag Pile, a game in which the Barons came back to score eight runs after two were out in the ninth inning to shock Atlanta, 8-7. The young man was hooked. He vowed that someday he—from Birmingham, Alabama, by way of Gerakeon Sparta, Greece—would own the Barons. A faintly familiar saga would unfold.

The hustling young immigrant made his fortune in America, first in the restaurant business and then in the hotel trade. In 1943, Jebeles sold his interests and became a man of leisure. But he had never abandoned his boyhood dream of owning the Barons, and after watching the Reds organization field poor teams and fare poorly at the gate for several years, Jebeles decided that the view from his regular box seat was not good enough anymore.

"If the Barons are for sale, I will come back owning the club," Jebeles declared before leaving Birmingham for Cincinnati. He was as good as his word, and local ownership of the franchise returned to Birmingham, just in time for the postwar baseball boom.

Jebeles proved a conscientious owner, intent on returning the Barons to prominence in the Southern Association. Unfortunately, "Mr. Jeb" knew nothing of the business of baseball and found himself saddled with a second-division club that did not draw well, even as Southern Association attendance nearly doubled during the 1946 season.

Jebeles admired Rick Woodward, who had provided Birmingham with winning baseball and a first-class ballpark. The Greek businessman wanted to be the same type of owner. Like Woodward, Jebeles eventually decided that by hiring a trusted subordinate, a "baseball man" with experience running a team, to handle the day-to-day operations of the Barons, he could give his adopted hometown the baseball prestige that had deserted the Magic City more than a decade earlier.

Gus Jebeles went to the annual minor league meeting in Los Angeles following the 1946 season looking for a general manager. Jebeles knew that if he failed to find an enterprising boss for his ball club, he might be forced to sell the Barons, and the dream of his youth would end in sour disappointment. At the Los Angeles meeting, Jebeles asked Frank Longinotti, the successful general manager of the Memphis Chicks, to recommend a man to save his Birmingham Barons.

"The man you are looking for is in this hotel, and I advise you to bid high for his services," said Longinotti in nominating Eddie Glennon for the open Birmingham job. Jebeles allowed the forty-three-year-old Glennon, then GM for a Wilmington, Delaware, team owned by the DuPonts, to name his own salary. It was a bargain for Jebeles, no matter how much Eddie Glennon set him back. The likable front-office wizard brought boom times back to Rickwood.

Eddie Glennon was a tough Irish kid from Philly. As a child, Eddie hung around Shibe Park, and several of Connie Mack's stars actually roomed at the boardinghouse run by Eddie's grandmother. The young Irishman apparently made an impression on Cornelius

Walt Dropo connects on massive homer "over the scoreboard" for 1948 Dixie Series Champions

McGillicuddy, whose parents had both been born on the Emerald Isle. Mack gave the adult Eddie a job in the Athletics' front office. By the time Glennon found his calling in baseball, he had already played professional football for 11 years, including a stint with the Frankford Yellow Jackets of the early NFL, and had managed a barnstorming championship basketball team.

In Wilmington, Glennon had made a name for himself as a franchise builder. He went into a town that had not had professional baseball in nineteen years and put together a team that drew 145,000 in its first year. Birmingham, by comparison, had only 74,000 paying customers that same season.

Glennon's impact on Birmingham baseball was immediate. He had a genius for promotion, and he worked tirelessly to link Birmingham civic pride to his baseball organization, stirring the embers of the fierce love of the game once embodied by Rick Woodward himself.

The record shows that his teams never enjoyed the on-field success of Woodward's outfits of the '20s and '30s. In his fifteen years as GM, only one of Glennon's ball clubs took the Southern Association pennant, though thanks to the league's Shaughnessy playoff system, the Barons did claim three Dixie Series titles against the champions of the Texas League. Eddie Glennon did, however, put successful, entertaining teams on the field in the '40s and '50s. These teams, which came very close to achieving Connie Mack's ideal of always contending for pennants but never actually winning one (Mack knew that a pennant meant higher player salaries, while a contender meant big paying crowds), finished second six times in Glennon's tenure.

In 1947, the first season of the Glennon era, Birmingham more than doubled its attendance of the previous year, even though the Barons finished in the second division with a record of 73-90. The third-place club of 1948 set the all-time attendance record in the Southern Association, with 445,926 fans attending seventy-seven home dates. These figures, it should be noted, do not include the additional 65,000 ladies' day admissions or the 95,000 fans who watched as the Barons triumphed in the playoffs and the Dixie Series, bringing the total number of fans who watched the Birmingham Barons in 1948 to well over 600,000—an astonishing total in a city with a metropolitan population of less than 300,000.

It should also be noted that this attendance record was based on the number of fans who actually—and eagerly—spun the turnstiles at Rickwood, rather than the number of tickets sold (plus season tickets), the basis upon which attendance is recorded in the "modern" era.

Dr. John Sherrill was a fixture at the park, sitting in the same seat at every game. And heckling Harold Seilor sat next to the tunnel to the visitors' dugout, baiting Chicks and Pelicans without mercy with a voice that carried across the entire park.

They sat in the bleachers all the way down the third-base foul line and paid fifty cents to sit in the low bleachers called "Glennon's Garden" in front of the scoreboard in left center. In those golden years, it was not a question of if you were going to Rickwood, it was a question of how early you could get there to get a good seat.

Several factors contributed to Glennon's success. The Irishman's early days in Birmingham coincided with a general baseball boom in the South, as the Southern Association topped the magical two-million mark in total attendance in both 1947 and 1948, for the only times in its sixty-one-year history. Secondly, realizing the crowd-pleasing glamour of the home run, Glennon moved the fences at Rickwood a second time in 1948, resulting in higher home run totals in the still-spacious Rickwood. Norm Zauchin thrilled Barons fans with 35 homers in 1950, a Birmingham record that stood for 37 years. Interestingly, the 6'5" Zauchin was a right-handed power hitter, unlike earlier Rickwood sluggers who had operated almost exclusively from the left-handed batter's box. Previously, most homers in Birmingham had been drives pulled tight down the right-field line to the relatively close bleachers. Glennon had changed the character of Rickwood by moving the fence, along with the ever-looming scoreboard, closer to home plate. And the success of the Atlanta Crackers, the so-called "Yankees of the Minors," gave the Barons a nearby rival to compete against in league standings and attendance figures.

Glennon spearheaded a number of projects designed to solidify Rickwood's reputation as the finest park in the South. He demolished the original Rickwood dugouts in 1950 to make room for a number of prime box seats along the first and third baselines. The dugouts were relocated farther down the baselines and lowered beneath ground level so as to not obstruct the fans' view of action on the field.

Also, in 1950, The Dugout restaurant was opened at Rickwood, marking a step toward Glennon's ultimate goal—a ballpark that served as an entertainment center for the whole family. In some ways, this was a precursor to the very desirable "mixed-use developments" that all pro teams seem to want to control near their venues. The Battery next to the Braves' stadium is the ultimate example of this.

Special "Ladies' Day" promotions were another example of his push to broaden the appeal of the Barons. An additional, larger ladies' room was added to Rickwood in 1948 to handle the increase in female attendance brought by his promotions. Glennon wanted to build a solid foundation for Rickwood's future—a future that seemed very bright in 1950, after four years in which the Barons had drawn the four largest seasonal gates in Birmingham history. The park was alive year-round. The Harlem Globetrotters played at Rickwood on a temporary court laid across the infield. Daredevils performed stunts for hushed crowds in the grandstand. And Rickwood still hosted football on occasion, primarily high school games.

Once again, Rickwood was ahead of its time. This time, it acted as a multiuse facility, a trend in pro sports that began in the 1960s and peaked in the 1970s with the "doughnut" stadiums in Atlanta, Cincinnati, Philadelphia, Pittsburgh, San Francisco, and St. Louis. As far as MLB and the NFL go, that was a trend better left in the past.

Almost 20,000 fans pack Rickwood at night to attend the 1955 Southern Association All Star Game

As Glennon settled in at Rickwood Field, he wasn't concerned about what was going to happen on Candlestick Point one day. He just knew it made economic—and community—sense to host lots of events. The old men who sat behind home plate smoking cigars knew his name and liked him for a job well done. He had a great position in a great baseball town—the "capital of the minor leagues." It was a good life in a good time for Eddie Glennon.

CHAPTER 14

A REAL AMERICAN HOLY PLACE

Many observers of American life and culture have noted the similarities between baseball and religion. Some have gone so far as to state that baseball *is* a religion, complete with a litany of faith—The Babe's Called Shot, Lou Gehrig's Farewell, Bobby Thomson's "The Giants Win the Pennant!" Home Run; a canon of saints—Ruth, Cobb, Paige, Wagner, Mays, and Mantle, and a select list of high holy sites—Wrigley Field, Fenway Park, Dodger Stadium, and Yankee Stadium.

If baseball is a religion, Rickwood Field is a shrine, a heaven on earth for the serious baseball fan. From its earliest days, Rickwood played host to the immortals of the game as they honed and displayed the skills that would take many to Cooperstown. Major league clubs frequently stopped off in Birmingham, a busy railroad hub, on the way north after spring training to play exhibition games against the Barons or other big-league teams.

Because teams from both the American and National Leagues played exhibitions at Rickwood, Birmingham fans actually had a better chance of seeing all of the top players of the era than residents of some cities in the majors. For example, a resident of Cincinnati in 1911 could see all the National League stars when they faced the hometown Reds, but the Cincy fan never got to see the greatest player in baseball since Ty Cobb played for the American League's Detroit Tigers, as this was long, long before interleague play.

Fans at Rickwood, however, did see Cobb in 1911, and in many subsequent appearances.

He tripled and singled in his first game in the new ballpark, but also made an error. Over the years, Cobb became friendly, or at least as friendly as Cobb could be, with Rick Woodward, and often hunted at the Barons owner's Alabama camp—until a falling-out between the two men over Ty's lack of regard for hunting laws.

Ty Cobb and Rogers Hornsby -- the all-time leading hitters in their leagues -- meet at Rickwood in 1923

Christy Mathewson played at Rickwood. In fact, the "Big Six" had distinct problems pitching in Rickwood Field, getting roughed up by the minor league Barons on a number of occasions. Perhaps the Birmingham boys remembered Mathewson's earlier, uncomplimentary remarks about the Magic City and seized the opportunity to embarrass the fading Matty.

They certainly had plenty of chances to get even with Matty. Manager John McGraw, who took the New York Giants to Mobile to train, made a point of playing an exhibition in Birmingham each year, and he also made a point of pitching Mathewson against the grudge-holding locals. Before the days of multimillion-dollar endorsements and commercials, the size of the crowd at the gate was everything—and the owners knew how to get the crowd to the park.

An aging Honus Wagner arrived on Birmingham's West End with the Pittsburgh Pirates in 1915. Visiting with Rick Woodward, the 41-year-old Flying Dutchman pointed to the young hurler working for the Barons and declared that the kid had great potential. The young pitcher was Burleigh Grimes.

A remarkable *Birmingham Age-Herald* photograph from 1923 shows a powerful, confident Rogers Hornsby, to many the greatest right-handed hitter ever, shaking hands with Ty Cobb, the greatest left-handed hitter ever (before an allegedly steroid-enhanced Barry Bonds came along), before a match between Hornsby's Cardinals and Cobb's Tigers at Rickwood.

In the previous season, both Cobb and Hornsby had hit .400. The *Age-Herald* photo documents an extremely rare baseball meeting. Hornsby, just shy of twenty-seven and with his greatest years in front of him, hit a massive homer that day, deep over the center-field fence, perhaps the longest hit at Rickwood to that time. Cobb, who in the photograph looks older than his thirty-six years, did not play as well as the Cardinals' second baseman, and his numbers in his remaining seasons show a decline in production.

The newspaper photograph captures a passage in American baseball. Under the title "Diamond Kings meet in Birmingham," the coronation of one king—Hornsby—and the deposition of another—Cobb—is recorded.

Babe Ruth wth young fans at Rickwood in 1933

The real king of baseball and all of American sports of the era was Babe Ruth. The Yankees and the Bambino were frequent visitors to Rickwood, and Ruth usually pleased the Birmingham fans by knocking baseballs into the relatively friendly right-field stands. His flair for the dramatic was in evidence during his Birmingham exhibitions, as reported by *The Age-Herald* of March 31, 1925:

> *It was a dramatic moment when the mighty slugger stepped to the plate with the sacks fully populated and his own team two runs in the rear. And then the Babe delivered in true Ruthian style, the drive going in a line over the right field wall—and four pairs of hoofs dented the plate.*

While the white Barons hosted a Cooperstown parade, the legends of the Negro Leagues faced the Black Barons in Birmingham. Oscar Charleston patrolled the outfield and later managed in Rickwood. Josh Gibson blasted homers to distant left center field. "Kool Kind Papa" Bell, as he was identified in *The Birmingham Reporter* (his Hall of Fame plaque calls James Thomas Bell "Cool Papa"), used his lightning speed to steal bases and make sensational defensive plays in the field.

And in 1945, Birmingham got a look at a player who would forever change the face of the game.

Jackie Robinson, the young star of the Kansas City Monarchs, played well against the Black Barons, scoring the game-winning run in a 1-0 extra-inning game. (After manager Piper Davis' vehement and protracted objection, the game was ruled a draw due to an umpire's interference call.)

The war and the resulting manpower shortage slowed the flow of Cooperstown-bound traffic through Birmingham, but during the postwar period, the stars fell on Rickwood again.

HOME RUN SLUGGERS MEET—Ted Williams (left) and Ralph Kiner, home run sluggers for the Boston Red Sox and Pittsburgh Pirates respectively, pose for the camera Saturday at Rickwood.

"I like your bat," Ted told Kiner. "I like yours, too," Kiner said to Williams.

Before the game, Kiner took pictures of Williams with his movie camera. Williams has hit five home runs in the past three days.

Saturday's meeting between the Bosox and Bucs was the second in 20 years.

Ted Williams and Ralph Kiner at Rickwood, April 1950. Williams hit two homers in his Rickwood debut that spring.

Superlative hitter and Korean War flying ace Ted Williams found the park to his liking. His Boston Red Sox, for several years the Barons' parent club, played a number of spring games in Eddie Glennon's domain in the 1940s and '50s. When asked about the pleasures of hitting at Rickwood, Williams observed, "Here you could hear that good sound of the bat against the ball."

Williams frequently took the measure of the "Negro bleachers," as did another left-handed power hitter, Stan the Man Musial.

Musial's 1954 drive, completely over the right-field bleachers, was measured at 486 feet by Alf Van Hoose of *The Birmingham News*. It became a Magic City legend, a standard by which future Rickwood homers were measured.

Another baseball legend came to Birmingham in the spring of 1949 for a mock big-league contest, but not in uniform. Connie Mack, of course, had never worn a uniform while managing, and at eighty-six years of age, in his fifty-second year as a manager, a change was unlikely. Still ramrod straight in the Rickwood dugout, "Mr. Mack" reminisced with a young reporter about his role in the birth of the ballpark. Much as a country doctor might discuss the delivery of a child, Mack seemed proud of Rickwood, as he had a right to be.

As Mack took his final leave of the diamond he had laid out forty years before, seventeen professional teams in Alabama prepared for the upcoming season, a baseball diocese surrounding the South's mother church of baseball. The great players, drawn to the playground that Rick Woodward had built with the help of one of the game's foremost apostles, had inspired the fervor that filled the region with the spirit of baseball.

CHAPTER 15

A SCHOOLBOY FROM FAIRFIELD

In 1948, Birmingham burned with a baseball fever unmatched since the final glory days of Rick Woodward in the early 1930s. Eddie Glennon's Barons were contenders in a tough Southern Association.

Local sportswriters favorably compared the '48 Barons to legendary past teams such as the Elliott Bigelow-led '28 Barons and the Dixie Series championship clubs of '29 and '31. Big Walt Dropo, the Moose from Moosup, Connecticut, hit .359 with 102 RBIs in 118 games and launched 14 homers, including a massive shot over the Rickwood scoreboard that lives on in Magic City baseball lore. A historical marker halfway up the original concrete wall in distant left center field announces, "This marks the spot where Walt Dropo's blast hit the concrete wall 467 feet from home plate 1948."

X marks the spot where Walt Dropo's blast hit the outer concrete wall in 1948

Dropo later became famous for his sterling Rookie of the Year season for the Boston Red Sox in 1950, earned with a .322 average, 34 homers, and a league-leading 144 RBIs. George Wilson tied what was then the all-time Barons homer record of 27 (a record broken by Norm Zauchin's 35 round-trippers two years later), driving in 102 runs while hitting .335. Tommy O'Brien smashed 78 extra-base hits and drove in 137 runs, batting

.359 for the year. It was a talented, deep Birmingham squad which, despite finishing the season in third place, won the Association playoffs as well as the Dixie Series.

No team in Southern baseball history—prior to the arrival of the big leagues in Atlanta in 1966—ever played before more fans at home. As good as the '48 Barons were—and they were very good—it is possible that they were not the best team to call Rickwood home in that magical summer. When the Barons left town to appear in Atlanta's Ponce de Leon Park (its name pronounced in true Southern parlance like the Leon in Leon Spinks' name rather than in the fashion of the Spanish explorer), or Nashville's Sulphur Dell (named for a pungent smell that hung over the ballpark), the Black Barons of playing manager Lorenzo "Piper" Davis took the field.

The 1948 Birmingham Black Barons, champions of the Negro American League, were a team for the ages. It is arguable that the Black Barons of '48 were the most talented team in Birmingham baseball history. The obvious competitors for this mythical title are the 1967 Birmingham A's powered by Reggie Jackson, Joe Rudi, Rollie Fingers, and a number of other important cogs of the Oakland championship run in the early 1970s.

Black Baron Artie Wilson, the last man to bat .400 in any league, hit .402 to lead the Negro American League. Wilson would later be named by *The Ballplayers* "the top Negro League shortstop in the 1940s," which is interesting since most of Wilson's known games were played at second base. Player-manager Davis, who just might have been the greatest player ever at Rickwood (many who saw him insist that Davis

Willie Mays grew up at 216 57th Street in Fairfield, west of Rickwood Field. Sadly, it's abandoned and overgown now.

tops all other Birmingham performers) hit .353 with 34 extra-base hits in 76 games.

Davis' outstanding season was actually, in some respects, subpar. The powerful 6'3", 187-lb. infielder hit .378 in '49 and .383 in '50 before leaving the Black Barons to become the first Black ballplayer signed by the Boston Red Sox organization. His best shot at the bigs was ironically stifled by Dropo's wondrous freshman season for Boston.

Willie Mays at Rickwood as a Black Baron

But the one player most identified with the Birmingham Black Barons—more so than Satchel Paige, Mule Suttles, Lester Lockett, or even "Mr. Black Baron" Piper Davis—was just a teenage greenhorn in 1948. When the Negro American League began play in April, Willie Howard Mays Jr. was a sixteen-year-old high school junior in Fairfield, just down the street from Rickwood. By September, young Willie, nicknamed "Sonny Boy" by *The Birmingham World*, a local Black newspaper, was the starting center fielder of the NAL champions, hitting .262 in 28 games and flashing brilliance in the field.

The crowning moment of Mays' initial professional season came on September 23, 1948, in Kansas City. The Black Barons had captured the first half championship of the NAL, playing almost entirely without the services of Mays, who had to finish his spring semester of high school before joining the team. The Kansas City Monarchs, abandoned prior to the season by their longtime star, Satchel Paige, who jumped to the Cleveland Indians for a late shot at white major league glory, won the second half of the split season.

A seven-game series for the championship of the league began in Rickwood, where the Black Barons jumped out to a three-game lead. The NAL series then moved to Kansas City, and the Black Barons floundered. Their lead evaporated, and the Monarchs confidently took the field at Blues Stadium for the seventh-and-deciding game.

Birmingham Black Barons Bus in front of Rickwood Field

In the top of the ninth, with the score tied, the bases loaded, and two out, Willie Mays, missing classes in his senior year at Fairfield Industrial High School to play for a Negro League championship, stepped into the right-handed batter's box. If a boy stepped into the batter's box, a man stepped out of it, on his way to first with a game-winning infield single.

The Black Barons again faced the Homestead Grays in the Negro World Series, and once again, the team representing Birmingham lost. The season had been memorable, and the future looked bright for Piper Davis' brilliant squad. But powerful new forces were acting on Negro baseball and America. After Jackie Robinson of the Brooklyn Dodgers broke the National League color line in 1947, the Cleveland Indians signed the American League's first Black players, Larry Doby and Satchel Paige. Both had appeared in the great Birmingham baseball year of 1948 at Rickwood. The integration of the major leagues doomed the historic and colorful leagues of the Black Barons and Monarchs. Like the Chicago American Giants and Pittsburgh Crawfords, the great Black Barons team of 1948 slowly disintegrated as its stars were picked off one by one by white organized baseball.

Artie Wilson was the first to go, snapped up by the Cleveland Indians immediately after the Black Barons' pennant-winning year. In 1949, he dominated the Pacific Coast League, an outstanding minor league often called a "third major league" due to the quality of its players, leading the league with a .348 average and winning the stolen base title. Despite his heroics, Wilson ended up getting only a brief look in the big leagues with the New York Giants in 1951.

Three years older than Wilson and nearing age thirty when Jackie Robinson made the majors, Piper Davis had to wait until 1951 for his shot at "organized baseball." Even in his mid-thirties and past his prime, Davis performed brilliantly in the Pacific Coast League and felt satisfaction when he homered in front of the not-so-welcoming Boston fans during spring training. The call from the majors, however, never came.

Birmingham Black Barons in their locker room after winning the 1948 NAL pennant. Willie Mays is against the back wall.

Willie Mays played one more season and part of another for the Black Barons after the championship year. In '49, after missing all of the road games in the first half since he was still in high school, Willie raised his batting average to .311. In 1950, Mays was hitting .330 for Birmingham when, at his father's home at 5507 Avenue G in Fairfield, he signed a contract to play for the New York Giants. For twenty-two seasons beginning in 1951, Mays played for the Giants, eventually moving with them to San Francisco. He suited up for a twenty-third season for the Mets, returning to a New York that loved him.

His legend grew larger once he retired in 1973 and reached a crescendo when he passed away as MLB started its three-day event to honor him and all Negro Leaguers in Birmingham in June 2024. Mays slammed 660 homers, batted .302 lifetime, made innumerable sensational circus catches, played the game as no one—before or since—has played it, making it look easy and *fun*.

And that game—uniquely Willie Mays' game—was first seen at Rickwood Field in Birmingham.

CHAPTER 16

YEARS WITHOUT SUMMERS

The numbers in the beginning were discouraging but not alarming. In 1950, the Birmingham Barons' home attendance at Rickwood fell below 400,000, despite Norm Zauchin's record-setting 35 homers and a second-place finish. But local fan support remained strong, and the league's attendance figures, while down from the previous four seasons, remained at near-record levels. Eddie Glennon, always optimistic, expected the crowds to return.

But the downward trend continued. In 1947, the Southern Association recorded its all-time record attendance: 2,180,344. But from that year until 1960, crowds declined every year until, in 1959, the entire Southern League drew only 614,000 fans, in all probability less than the Barons drew for all their home games in 1948 alone.

While the Barons drew relatively well, attendance sank at Rickwood just as it had at the other Southern ballparks. By 1952, only 178,000 showed up for Birmingham's home schedule, less than half the total for any of the final three seasons of the 1940s. Occasionally during the 1950s, there was a rally, such as when the Barons won their first Southern Association pennant in twenty-seven years in 1958. But by 1961, Rickwood crowds had fallen dangerously close to pre-Glennon levels.

Even the Hot Stove League, the joyous gathering of Birmingham's baseball faithful at the Thomas Jefferson Hotel, began to dwindle.

In the initial year of the New Frontier, only 112,000 Barons faithful paid their way to sit in the recently installed box seats that had been purchased at a bargain from the historic Polo Grounds before the wrecking ball leveled New York's grand old ballpark.

There were, of course, a myriad of reasons for the decline and ultimate demise of the old Southern Association. Minor league baseball in general declined in popularity throughout the 1950s, as major league games became available on television. In the South, in particular, the new availability of air conditioning in homes hurt attendance on sizzling summer days and nights. Finally, and perhaps most important, the Southern Association never came to grips with the revolution in baseball after "the color line" had been broken.

Times were changing.

Even as fan interest in Birmingham baseball declined, outstanding players and teams performed at Rickwood Field. Jimmy Piersall hit in the .350s and made acrobatic catches for the Barons before heading to the Boston Red Sox, and often asked the hometown fans where they wanted him to hit the ball before he stepped into the batter's box. Bob Bruce, Phil Regan, and "Shakey Joe" Grzenda, so named for his nervous habit of chain smoking, all future big leaguers, provided outstanding pitching for the '58 pennant winners. In 1960, Stan Palys, a thirty-year-old journeyman, hit .373 and smacked 85 extra-base hits for the Barons. Pitcher Howie Koplitz went 23-3 for the '61 Barons, with a no-hitter along the way.

The Black Barons, fighting the stream of baseball history, survived the '50s, one of only four Negro League teams to do so. Outstanding talent still passed through the Negro Leagues. Young shortstops and future Hall of Famers Ernie Banks of the Kansas City Monarchs and Henry Aaron of the Indianapolis Clowns impressed fans as they came through Rickwood, hoping to follow Jackie Robinson to the bigs.

In 1958, the Birmingham Black Barons captured their final pennant in the Negro American League. Coincidentally, that was the same year the white Barons won the last of their seven Southern Association championships.

Although the 1958 pennant brought joy to Barons fans, the title brought concern to team officials. By winning their way into the Dixie Series, the Barons had come face-to-face with integration on the diamond. Both Austin and Corpus Christi—finalists for the Texas League championship—had Black players on their rosters, and Birmingham had a city ordinance that expressly prohibited sports competition between the races: (*emphasis added below*)

> Section 597, Negroes and Whites Not To Play Together.
> It shall be unlawful for a Negro and a White person to play together or in company with each other in any game of cards, dice, dominoes, checkers, *baseball*, softball, football, basketball, or similar game.

The city had faced a similar dilemma early in the fall of 1953. The Barons had a good chance to make the Dixie Series that year. Much to the dismay of the keepers of the segregated faith, integrated Texas League teams also had a shot at making the Dixie Series. To eliminate the possible confrontation, moderates on the City Commission, led by Mayor Jimmy Morgan, made clear their position on Ordinance 597: the statute was almost entirely unconstitutional and needed to be amended.

There was, in that fall of 1953, a very brief window for racial moderates in Birmingham to finally erase the baseball color line. That opportunity arose from a scandal that temporarily displaced longtime Public Safety Commissioner Eugene "Bull" Connor, the unrepentant racist who ran the Birmingham Police Department as his own personal army against societal change.

In December 1951, Connor suspended a high-ranking detective named Henry Darnell after Darnell implied that the Birmingham police chief (just under Connor in the chain of command) was running a protection racket for a prostitution operation. Darnell was outraged, and as a detective, he had the right skill set to get even with Connor, whose personal habits and proclivities he knew well.

On December 21, 1951, Darnell, accompanied by a reporter from the *Birmingham Post-Herald* and others, made a beeline through the Tutwiler Hotel in downtown Birmingham to the door of Room 706. He proceeded to pound on the door for twenty-three minutes. When the door finally opened, the occupants were revealed to be fifty-four-year-old Bull Connor and his thirty-four-year-old secretary.

In 1951, it was illegal in Birmingham for two people of the opposite sex not related by blood or marriage to be alone in a hotel room. Bull *was* married, but not to his secretary. He declined to run for re-election in 1953.

Although the Barons ultimately fell short of the 1953 Southern Association pennant (making the argument over Section 597 moot *for that specific series*), the door for integrated baseball had swung open like the door of Room 706 at the Tutwiler.

With Connor out of office until at least 1957, major league exhibition games (now fully integrated) quickly returned to Rickwood Field. The Milwaukee Braves of 1954, featuring rookie Henry Aaron, played a Rickwood exhibition against the Brooklyn Dodgers of Jackie Robinson and Roy Campanella on a truly bizarre stage. Approximately 5,000 Black fans overflowed the so-called Negro bleachers in right field and standing-room-only areas down both foul lines and around the outfield fence. Meanwhile, less than 2,000 fans occupied the 9,612 seats reserved for whites. The game was therefore played before a packed house, but the grandstand was practically empty!

In that same brief shining spring of 1954, the Musial-led St. Louis Cardinals (with former Birmingham Black Barons star Bill Greason on the roster) played at Rickwood against the Chicago White Sox. It was in this preseason series that Musial hit his famous tape-measure homer, remembered in Birmingham decades later.

But for Major League Baseball at Rickwood, April 1954 turned out to be a false spring, killed by a coldhearted electorate and leading to a long baseball winter of discontent. Six weeks after integrated baseball succeeded in Birmingham, *Brown v. Board of Education of Topeka* shocked white Birmingham into abject fear. A citywide referendum on Section 597 was held two weeks after the Supreme Court ruled in the landmark case and resulted in a three-to-one (19,640 votes to 6,685) defeat for baseball integration. Birmingham diamonds remained segregated.

The situation in 1958 was defused by an odd compromise. Corpus Christi, the winner of the Texas League pennant, obligingly agreed to substitute white players for the three Black players, including a starting third baseman, on their roster. Barons GM Eddie Glennon had indicated earlier that he would allow the Texas teams to substitute a white player (including major leaguers) for their Black players while in Birmingham. The Barons thus avoided ever *knowingly* competing against a racially mixed team at Rickwood Field during the sixty-one-year history of the Southern Association.

In the 1910s, the Barons had played exhibition games against the Cincinnati Reds, who featured a speedy Cuban outfielder named Armando Marsans. The Reds assured a nervous Birmingham baseball establishment that Marsans, along with another Cuban signee named Rafael Almeida who eventually played a number of seasons for the Barons, was a "genuine Caucasian," despite the fact that the Reds may or may not have known that each had one Black parent.

In late November 1961, Barons owner Albert Belcher, who had become a part owner of the team in 1949 and gained majority control in '58, attended a critical league meeting in Tampa, accompanied by Eddie Glennon. At that meeting, the Birmingham Barons, the franchise lovingly nurtured by Rick Woodward and idolized for decades by a city, died, a victim of the changing times and an unchanging Birmingham. The team refused to integrate and consequently pulled out of the league. The Southern Association itself folded in Tampa, and a grand part of the New South was gone forever.

Glennon had already resigned before attending the fateful meetings in Tampa. He had gone as a favor to Belcher. Glennon had already accepted a job with the Triple-A Denver Bears for the 1962 season. In fifteen years in Birmingham, the gregarious Irishman had seen everything: almost immediate success at the gate; a slow, agonizing decline; and finally, a painful death. Many men would be glad to leave, to get away from the bitter disappointment that comes when so much is won only to be lost. But Glennon loved Birmingham and baseball, was saddened to leave the Magic City, and was heartbroken that he was taking baseball with him.

There was no baseball in Birmingham in 1962 or '63, save for the tattered remnants of the Black Barons that sporadically appeared at Rickwood, ironically given continuous life by the dark forces of segregation and Jim Crow. It was during this time that the worst racial violence of the civil rights era forever fixed the image of Birmingham in the national mind. Perhaps if there had been baseball at Rickwood that terrible summer of 1963—baseball to make hearts see light, to ease tensions on steamy Birmingham nights—understanding and compromise, rather than police dogs and bombs, might be what we remember of that Birmingham summer. Of course, in a baseball sense, there was no summer at all in Birmingham in 1963.

CHAPTER 17

RUMPLED, CHILDISH SOULS WHO GO TO GAMES FOR FREE: RICKWOOD'S ROOFTOP LEGENDS

Baseball, perhaps more than any other sport, has been closely connected to the writers and broadcasters covering it. George Vecsey, a top sports columnist who also won fame collaborating with Alabama and Southern favorite Loretta Lynn on her autobiography *Coal Miner's Daughter*, described his sports media brethren this way in *A Year in the Sun* (critically, yes but maybe more lovingly that is instantly apparent): "Sportswriters? The way the word is usually used, when introduced to strangers, it takes on the condescending sound of a rumpled, childish soul who goes to games for free ... bitches about the high salaries of athletes, and stumbles through the week ill-dressed, ill-conditioned and hung over. Oscar Madison in The Odd Couple is a sportswriter."

Newspaper reporters and radio broadcasters fed the world its information one word at a time until the appearance of affordable television. Sitting high above the field, the men who covered the action at Rickwood relied on the power of their words and the excitement in their voices to create the images of the game.

And at a time when Birmingham's self-image was derived, at least in part, by the success and failure of its baseball teams against the rest of the world, their words mattered mightily. The original press box at Rickwood was a small, open-air gazebo perched on the roof high behind home plate. A single flagpole in the center carried the flags whose colors faded quickly, baked by the Birmingham sun.

As baseball captured the passions of Birmingham and an entire nation, the tiny press box proved too small to accommodate the growing cadre of sportswriters, radio announcers and game officials on hand for the games at bustling Rickwood. In time, the original gazebo gave way to two small press boxes side by side. Then, additional radio booths were placed on either side.

The roof was a busy place, and the press box itself was particularly loud. It was a place of cigarette and cigar smoke. Clattering typewriters and excited play-by-play. Banter between friends. And profanity. And love of a game they were fortunate enough to cover for a living. With no owner's suite for officials, the roof was often the best seat in the house. It was the ultimate skybox.

Barons general manager Eddie Glennon was once thrown out of a game for baiting an umpire from his favorite folding chair on the roof. An unspoken responsibility for the chair jockeys up there was retrieving the balls that were fouled back onto the roof, then ignoring the fans below who begged and bellowed for the ball. Business was business, after all, and baseballs even then were expensive.

The balls that cleared the roof fence were gobbled up by the tiny mob of youths wearing their gloves and baseball caps in the hopes of taking home a souvenir. Some things about baseball have not changed at all.

Rick Woodward had a bit of the sportswriter in his soul. In 1934, longtime *Birmingham News* sports editor Zipp Newman asked the Barons owner to write his baseball memoirs. Woodward, delighted by the invitation, produced a sprawling account of the inner workings of the Birmingham Barons in the first third of the 20th century. Woodward's writing, though often disjointed and rambling, was ingratiating, self-effacing, and ultimately pleasing to the reader.

It was a style not unlike that of Woodward's friend, Zipp Newman. Zipp became sports editor of *The Birmingham News* at the time of Christ and served in that position until the second coming. Actually, it only seemed that way.

Newman actually headed *The News'* sports department from 1919 to 1959. More than any other man, Newman created the images of the great sports heroes of the golden '20s that live on in the popular mind of Birmingham to this day. When an old-time Alabama football fan "remembers the Rose Bowl," the memories are usually framed in the language and imagery of Zipp Newman.

What today's Auburn fan knows about the legendary Mike Donahue was probably gleaned from old copies of "Dustin' 'Em Off," Newman's daily column. And when Birmingham remembers the powerhouse Barons of Rick Woodward's Southern Association dynasty, its memories are tinted by his unabashed boosterism and his hyperbolic style. The hardworking editor loved Birmingham and the sports he covered, and it showed in every overheated line he penned.

Zipp Newman was a character right out of a 1930s newspaper movie. He knew the sports immortals: Ruth. Dempsey. Jones. Tilden. Newman hobnobbed with the powerful moguls of the sports world as well as the leading citizens in Birmingham. He spent his extra time out at Rickwood scoring Black Barons games, where he was one of the first white men to "discover" a talented young pitcher named Satchel Paige. He even found time to invent a football board game (which Parker Brothers rejected). When Newman "retired" in 1959 (actually, he continued to write a column for another fifteen years), young Benny Marshall took the reins of *The News'* sports department and directed the coverage of baseball and Rickwood Field for the next ten years.

Birmingham was lucky. During some of the darkest days in the city's history, depressed readers could turn to the sports page and escape into the daily column by Marshall, one of the most gifted sportswriters to ever transform a simple ballgame into an epic battle.

A critic once noted that Benny Marshall wrote about sports contests "as if they were the Peloponnesian Wars." But to say that Marshall was a sportswriter is akin to saying that Mark Twain wrote funny stories.

His talent had been apparent even when he was a boy. He had graduated from Howard College before he turned twenty. Published pieces of his writing had appeared when he was fifteen. He had, as Roy Hobbs had, a "gift," a gift that Birmingham would enjoy for thirty-five years but that would eventually destroy him.

At his best, Benny used sportswriting as a cover. What he really wrote about were dreams and disappointments and despair. The writer was intimately acquainted with his subjects, and it showed. But there were demons inside him, demons that would haunt his steps and bedevil his great mind until he shot himself in 1969 when he was only forty-nine years old.

Birmingham News sportswriter Clyde Bolton wrote in 1993 that people still asked him why Benny Marshall killed himself. Bolton said that he did not know, but we think we do.

Only a few years before his death, Benny Marshall wrote a piece titled "September Memory." It is ostensibly about the Dizzy Dean-Ray Caldwell showdown in the 1931 Dixie Series. But "September Memory" is really about the time when he loved life at Rickwood Field and his Birmingham Barons, and when he had a father and a brother and the world made sense.

The heartbreaking conclusion of "September Memory" foreshadows the end of Benny's life. In it, Marshall mentions that his father had died (he does not tell the reader that his father committed suicide in front of the young Benny), and he recalls the death of his brother on Iwo Jima.

And then, in a haunting, beautiful finish, middle-aged Benny Marshall revealed the depth of his depression by comparing his life and time to that of the boy he had been:

> *I think now that there had to be many fathers who left work, then came home on September 16, 1931 in Birmingham with songs in the voices that lighted the eyes of their sons because Ray Caldwell had won. And this surely was the happiest day anyone had ever known anywhere. That's the way it was with baseball then.*

Alf Van Hoose, already a veteran sportswriter by 1969, took over as sports editor after Marshall's death. The dark clouds that had covered Birmingham and engulfed Benny Marshall began to clear during Van Hoose's tenure as head of the area's largest sports department.

The gregarious Van Hoose was a serious baseball man. Even if the exploits of the Black Barons and the Negro League stars would not earn attention from the media establishment of the time, Van Hoose personally served as the Black Barons' official game scorer. He was a popular figure at the ballpark and brought back some of the boosterism that had characterized Zipp Newman's work.

His staff included Paul Hemphill, later a best-selling author whose book on minor league baseball, *Long Gone*, was made into a movie. At the time, though, Hemphill was a young journalist with what seemed to many the dream job of covering the beloved Barons and the Southern League pennant races.

Van Hoose's positive coverage of the fledgling Barons of the early 1980s proved invaluable to a new team trying to establish itself in an environment that had proved hostile to baseball only a few years before—and one that faced the difficulty of inevitable comparisons with the great baseball legends that had thrilled Birmingham fans since 1910.

The most famous, or perhaps more accurately, the most notorious radio broadcaster covering the Barons was Eugene "Bull" Connor. He parlayed his fame as the radio voice of the splendid Birmingham championship teams of the '30s and '40s into a political career that left a seemingly indelible imprint of the city of Birmingham in the minds of the entire world.

Bull, whose nickname came from his booming voice and his trademark call of "ooooouuuutttt," became the head of Birmingham's police force primarily because voters liked the way he called a baseball game. For several hours a day, several days a week, Bull Connor had the undivided attention of most of Birmingham year after year. In the early days, he worked matinees, relying on only the cold statistics of the Western Union ticker tape to re-create the action for the fans at home, imaginatively filling in the picture with his enthusiastic voice and sound effects machine. In this way, he was like the young Ronald Reagan, who broadcast games in Iowa based on wire reports and sound effects. But Reagan and Connor bore few other traits in common, especially regarding race relations.

Gabby Bell manned the volume control of the crowd noise for Bull before later going on to establish himself as the voice of the Barons for a generation of baseball-hungry listeners who followed their Barons while they bused from town to town throughout the South. Gabby's famous assistant in the booth during his tenure behind the microphone was Stretch Martin, a very colorful but altogether fictitious character invented by Bell.

This was long before the days of equal time in media, so few could compete with Bull's public persona when he decided to run for elected office.

Much of Birmingham's modern tragedy embedded in our nation's memory is inextricably linked to this most exuberant of baseball broadcasters who, unfortunately, did not stick to broadcasting baseball for a living. Through the years, the impressions that many Birmingham fans had of Rickwood Field and the events that took place there came filtered through the announcers and sportswriters who brought the games to the front porches of Woodlawn and West End during the Alabama summers. As time passed, these men—Zipp, Benny, Bull, Gabby, Van Hoose, Hemphill, Naylor Stone, Bob Phillips, Wayne Martin, Clyde Bolton, and all the others—became part of Rickwood Field, just as Connie Mack's diamond and Rick Woodward's grandstand are a part of the West End ballpark.

CHAPTER 18

CHARLIE O. AND REGGIE

Charles Oscar Finley got his start in baseball as a batboy for Rick Woodward's Barons in the early 1930s. Eventually, "Charlie O." became a ballplayer himself until he contracted tuberculosis in 1946. Narrowly escaping death, Finley decided to give up baseball. Apparently inspired by his experience, he went into the life insurance business.

Finley built an empire in the Chicago insurance market. By age forty, he was a multimillionaire, bored and looking for new worlds to conquer. He decided to return to baseball, but this time on the major league level. Finley wanted to own a big-league club, and he wanted to run it, too.

His first effort to obtain a ball club, the Kansas City Athletics, was thwarted when Arthur Johnson outbid him. But Johnson died a few months later, and in 1960, forty-two-year-old Charlie Finley had his own personal plaything, the Athletics franchise. He would hold it for the next twenty-one years, and it would be one hell of a ride. By 1964, a chastened Birmingham wanted baseball back and was willing to integrate its team to regain the sport. Finley, fondly remembering the full houses at the Rickwood of his youth, determined to put a farm club from his organization in Rickwood.

The new team—playing in the "new" Southern League, an integrated circuit made up of teams from the old Southern Association and South Atlantic League—was originally called the Barons. But after a one-year layoff in 1966, when Al Belcher, again the local franchise owner, retired from baseball—selling Rickwood (and the right to deal with Finley) to the city—the Barons took on the name of the parent club, becoming the Birmingham A's. The price the city paid for the stadium? $365,000.

Mayor Albert Boutwell's papers, now in the Birmingham Public Library Archives, contain numerous letters from local citizens, prophetically reminding the mayor about the magical history of the park and what a tragedy it would be to lose it.

The Birmingham A's, in their eleven-year run at Rickwood (including two years in which they were called Barons) never played before Glennon-sized crowds. But the franchise produced more fine big-league players in one three-year stretch (1967-69) than Glennon's Barons produced in fifteen seasons. The stars of three consecutive World Series championship teams—the Oakland A's of 1972-74—honed their skills on the Rickwood diamond in the late 1960s.

The 1967 Birmingham A's featured two players who were enshrined in the Baseball Hall of Fame just a few years after their retirement from the big leagues. Rollie Fingers, then a starting pitcher (and without the trademark handlebar mustache), came on strong late in'67, recovering remarkably from an Opening Day line drive to the face. He returned to Birmingham to compile a strong 10-4 record in '68. But the player who grabbed the headlines and most of the attention of knowledgeable observers at Rickwood was a twenty-one-year-old outfielder named Reginald Martinez Jackson.

Even at the Double-A level of the minors, there was something magical about Jackson that placed him at the center of championship teams. The '67 A's dominated the six-team Southern League, going 84-55 to easily capture the pennant. Reggie, despite missing a healthy portion of the season on weekend duty with the parent A's (he played 25 games in the bigs that year), hit .293 with 60 extra-base hits—17 homers, 17 triples, and 26 doubles. The .293 average and 26 doubles were matched by another Birmingham outfielder who would find stardom in Oakland: Joe Rudi. Several other future big leaguers, including power-hitting third baseman Sal Bando, catcher Dave Duncan, and shortstop Bert Campaneris, populated the Birmingham A's roster of manager John McNamara, a field leader who later starred as the skipper of the 1986 pennant-winning Boston Red Sox.

The 1967 season in Birmingham was notable not only for the way it ended—a pennant, Birmingham's first in nine years—but for how it began. The official first pitch to start the season, which actually came a week into the season because of scheduling difficulties, was thrown by actress Mamie Van Doren and caught by a squatting Charlie O. Finley behind the plate.

This poster hangs at Regions Field to honor Reggie Jackson, the star of the 1967 Barons

If you search something inane like "1950s biggest sex symbols," you'll invariably find a photo of the shapely Van Doren. And here she was on the same sacred mound used by Satchel Paige, Christy Mathewson, and Dizzy Dean, through an odd sequence of events. In the early '60s, Mamie had been a constant companion of Los Angeles Angels pitcher Bo Belinsky. When their relationship fizzled, the thirty-ish Mamie took up with a nineteen-year-old Angels bonus-baby pitcher named Lee Meyers. The starstruck Meyers married the actress after a whirlwind courtship, even appearing on the Johnny Carson show with Mamie to give the breathless details of their romance.

The glitzy marriage was not good for Meyers' career with the

Angels, who shipped him to the A's organization. Young Lee was assigned to Birmingham to start the 1967 season, and the Hollywood-to-Rickwood connection resulted in Mamie's Night Out at

BIRMINGHAM ATHLETICS, 1967 SOUTHERN LEAGUE CHAMPIONS

Front row—L. Bragan, batboy; McNamara, Jr., batboy; Lee, ballboy, D. Bragan, batboy. Middle row — Jackson, Miranda, Frati, Lauzerique, McNamara, manager; Bowlin, Davidson, Taylor, Dobbins, Handrahan. Back row—Rosario, Guzek, Duncan, Wojcik, Rudi, Grzenda, Blanco, Fingers, Olivo, Norton, Lachemann, Garrett, trainer.

1967 Southern League Champion Birmingham A's - One of the greatest teams ever in the minors

Rickwood Field. A local sportswriter came up with an immortal line to describe what Mamie Van Doren hurled at Charlie O. that April night.

"It just had to be a curve."

The union of Lee Meyers, Birmingham lefthander, and the movie sex symbol ended disastrously. Mamie dumped the young ballplayer, and his career, once so promising, went nowhere. Meyers never pitched an inning in the big leagues. He died at age twenty-six in a high-speed car crash.

While his pitching career was unspectacular, Meyers is remembered for a much nobler reason. He was specifically mentioned by Jackson upon his return to Rickwood for the momentous event MLB staged there in 2024. Reggie singled out teammates Rudi, Fingers, Duncan, and Meyers as being instrumental in helping him survive the intense racism hurled his way during his summer in

Birmingham in 1967.

Throughout the '60s, Charlie O. continued the stream of talent through Rickwood Field. Vida Blue, only two years away from glory as the American League MVP and Cy Young Award winner in 1971, wowed Birmingham fans with a 10-3 record in just over half a season in Rickwood. On the mound, the nineteen-year-old phenom looked a bit like another young Birmingham pitcher of the past, Satchel Paige. Gene Tenace, later a World Series MVP, hit .324 with 21 homers in 90 games for Birmingham in 1969—an impressive power performance in pitcher-friendly Rickwood.

As the decade ended, however, the Birmingham A's went into a decline. The talent level dropped precipitously as Finley, hamstrung by baseball rules on buying players, no longer had a stockpile of bonus babies to dole out to his farm clubs. The minor leagues were increasingly a training ground for young talent rather than an exercise in building winning teams. Fan loyalty to constantly changing teams with new faces was erratic at best. After 1970, the Birmingham A's never had another winning season. Attendance, which had leveled off at around 50,000 between 1967 and 1969, fell to as low as a mere 21,000 fans in 1973.

There were a few bursts of glory as the old ballpark struggled to survive. In 1974, the Atlanta Braves visited for an exhibition against an excellent Baltimore Orioles team. Managed by Earl Weaver, the Orioles had won four pennants in the previous decade and boasted multiple Hall of Famers including Jim Palmer and Brooks Robinson. But the capacity crowd that packed Rickwood on that April 2 were there to see Mobile, Alabama, native Hank Aaron, who would break Babe Ruth's all-time home run record six days later in Atlanta.

Aaron had faced ugly racist intimidation throughout the later years of his lonely struggle to catch the Babe. But in Birmingham, in a spring only a decade removed from the "Bombingham" of police dogs and Bull Connor, Aaron was given a hero's welcome by his fellow native Alabamians. Though much work remained, an amazing amount of healing had been done, especially on the diamond.

The dreaded news, thought to be inevitable by many baseball

people, came to Birmingham after the 1975 season. The Birmingham A's were moving up I-59 to become the latest incarnation of the Chattanooga Lookouts. Rickwood was vacant for the second time in a dozen years, and this time, many believed the old ballpark would never open its gates again.

A semipro outfit (more "semi" than "pro") called the Alabama Barons attempted to resurrect baseball in Rickwood in 1978. But the demeaning effort only served to show how much the "best baseball town in the South" had fallen. The Freedom League, in which this short-lived version of the Barons played, folded after only three games.

Summers came and went. Rickwood, the home of legends, the baseball cathedral, began to rot. The musty smell of cigar smoke faded. The old ballpark seemed certain to go the way of Ponce de Leon Park in Atlanta, Sulphur Dell in Nashville, and Russwood Park in Memphis—all, like Rickwood, with prominent roles in Negro Leagues history. Those three had given way to the wrecking ball or the elements.

Baseball may be timeless, but time had become Rickwood's enemy.

CHAPTER 19

INDIAN SUMMER

Birmingham advertising executive John Forney was best known as "The Voice of the Crimson Tide" for his years announcing the gridiron contests of the University of Alabama. For this he earned a plaque in the Alabama Sports Hall of Fame. But Forney also played a major role in the resurrection of Rickwood Field in the early 1980s.

Forney approached Jules Arden Clarkson ("please call me Art") in 1979 with the idea of bringing baseball back to Birmingham. It was a prescient choice, because perhaps no other man could have succeeded in the task at hand. Art Clarkson was a man of unique talents.

In 1979, Clarkson was the general manager of the Memphis Chicks of the Southern League. He had built a successful Double-A franchise in the same city where Triple-A baseball had failed two years earlier. He was a showman, a genuine sports personality of the old school.

He had learned through hard experience what made minor league sports teams winners on and off the field. Clarkson was born in Chicago, but grew up in Los Angeles, where he spent his summers rooting for the Hollywood Stars at old Gilmore Field. Art loved baseball, but as he later said, "I guess I was better at hitting other people than hitting a ball."

Young Art, tall and rangy, played college football for Cal State Northridge before turning pro in the old Continental Football League of the mid-1960s. A knee injury in 1965 ended his playing days, and he returned to California and entered the insurance business.

By 1973, Art Clarkson had it made. Business was booming. His natural knack for making money assured his future success. But

Art wanted to get back into sports, and when an opportunity to sell season tickets for the Southern California Sun of the new World Football League presented itself, Clarkson jumped at the chance.

Once inside the business of sports, Clarkson's ascent was rapid, as he showed an amazing ability to land on his feet when fate gave him a heave. When the WFL folded in 1975, Clarkson, at that time in charge of ticket sales for the Memphis Southmen franchise, got a job in baseball with the Memphis Blues, a Triple-A franchise. He had an opportunity to become the GM of the Blues when boss Denny McLain (the majors' last 30-game winning pitcher in 1968 for Detroit) quit under pressure in 1976. But Art turned down the job, recommending that the team fold. He knew he needed more experience in baseball before taking control of a franchise.

Clarkson went to Tidewater of the International League as an assistant GM for one season. After that single year, Clarkson headed back to Memphis to become the boss of the city's brand-new Southern League franchise.

His record at Memphis was nothing short of phenomenal. In his first season, his Memphis Chicks drew 150,000 fans to Double-A baseball in the same ballpark where Triple-A couldn't attract 100,000 paying customers.

In Art's second year, attendance zoomed to 250,000, and in 1980, the Chicks, still using Clarkson's methods, played to 320,000. By 1980, Art Clarkson was gone from Memphis. He had become intrigued with Birmingham and Rickwood Field, and the operator in him longed for a piece of the ownership action in the ball club he ran.

While still at Memphis, he had driven with friends on a Sunday afternoon to Birmingham to take a look at the old ballpark. Finding it locked up, Art scaled a fence and walked out onto the field. He found himself overcome with emotion.

A baseball history buff, Art Clarkson knew about the long history of Rickwood. He knew about the great players who had excelled there, of the great games that had been played there. Standing on Connie Mack's diamond, perhaps picturing Cobb slashing spikes high into third, the Babe tiptoeing around the bases after a mammoth homer, or Mays cavorting in center, Clarkson made up his mind.

He would bring baseball back to Rickwood.

Skepticism greeted the October 1980 announcement of the return of the Birmingham Barons to Rickwood with Art as GM and part owner. Few believed that a successful minor league team could operate anymore in Birmingham, and fewer believed that fans could be attracted to the dilapidated park, which was now seventy years old and more than showing her age.

But Clarkson beat the odds. His first Barons team attracted 220,000 fans, the largest Rickwood attendance in thirty years. By 1983, when the Barons won the first pennant in sixteen years for Birmingham, over 250,000 fans crowded into the old ballpark.

Art used the same methods he had perfected in Memphis to bring fans out to the West End playground. He updated and refurbished the ballpark. Over the outcry of Rickwood traditionalists, he constructed an exploding message board after tearing down the historic mechanical scoreboard.

Clarkson did whatever it took to attract the fans of the high-flying 1980s to the gentlemanly pace of the game of baseball in one of its oldest venues. He engaged in clever, popular promotions geared for the minor league market. Art also knew the basic value of fielding winning teams.

He canceled his working agreement with the Detroit Tigers when the parent club did not send him top-flight ballplayers and switched his affiliation to the Chicago White Sox. And his ball clubs did win, capturing two last pennants to be painted on the faded north wall of Rickwood during the team's seven-season tenure. A new generation of outstanding ballplayers, the best and brightest in Rickwood since the talented Birmingham A's squads of the late 1960s, powered Clarkson's best ball clubs.

Third baseman Howard Johnson and outfielder Glenn Wilson, both future big-league All-Stars, performed well for the '81 Barons. Future big leaguer Don Heinkel won 19 games for the pennant-winning 1983 Birmingham squad. Rondal Rollins slammed 39 homers in 1987 to set an all-time Barons record at Birmingham, with late help by a 6'5" righthander fresh out of Stanford. Jack McDowell, who would go on to snare the AL Cy Young Award in 1993, was instrumental in helping the Barons win another Southern League flag.

Clarkson was living his dream. He had a successful baseball team playing in a wonderful, historic ballpark. He had made Birmingham once more a "baseball town."

But even as he savored his improbable success, vampiric forces, forces that would suck the new life out of old Rickwood, were at work on the West End of Birmingham. Art had come to Rickwood Field because he loved the ballpark. Like all true baseball fans, he had an affinity for the romance of the bygone eras of the national pastime.

But by 1987, the cruel, violent forces of the late 20th century had muscled their way into his pinstriped baseball fantasy. The neighborhood surrounding Rickwood became harder and meaner during the 1980s. Happy fans exiting the ballpark became angry victims as they discovered that their cars had been vandalized.

The perception of an unsafe neighborhood had the effect of reality. Attendance, though still strong, gradually began to slump. In 1986, only 147,000 paid to see the Barons in Rickwood.

Clarkson appealed to Birmingham city officials for additional security in the Rickwood parking lot and an increased police presence in the ballpark's neighborhood. The Barons' GM felt that his problems were receiving little priority from City Hall, despite the obvious economic impact of a professional baseball franchise that could draw 250,000 people a year into a depressed area of the central city. The dream was fading.

He began examining his options. Ever the businessman, Clarkson was aware all along that he could make more money playing ball in one of Birmingham's affluent suburbs than in Rickwood. The continuing problems at the aging ballpark—the hassles with the city, the rising crime rate, the perception of decay—pushed the Barons boss to a painful end.

He decided to move his club to Hoover, a well-to-do suburb, and a park built especially for the Barons and to Clarkson's specifications. And so, Art Clarkson left behind the beautiful old ballpark and a portion of his soul in Birmingham's West End. At the end of the 1987 season, they turned off Jim Burt's lights after handing out certificates to the fans who attended the last Barons game at Rickwood Field.

Curt Bloom started a thirty-three-season run as the Barons play-by-play announcer in 1992 when the team was playing in Hoover. During a visit to Rickwood in 1996, he spotted something amazing. "The lineup from the last game ever played at Rickwood was still written in chalk on a board there. It was really crazy, but written at the bottom of it was a recognizable name. It said the starting pitcher that day was 'J. McDowell.' That's right—Jack McDowell threw the last game that the Barons played there."

So "Black Jack" McDowell and his teammates walked off Connie Mack's diamond that day, and the fans walked down the ramp out of Rick Woodward's grandstand. And the park stood quiet and empty except for the baseball memories that filled the stands. America's Oldest Ballpark hung onto hope that one day the crack of the bat would again be heard echoing off her bleachers.

The veritable old facility would again see life, but not with an everyday tenant.

CHAPTER 20

A TREE GROWS IN ATLANTA: HOW THE MOVIES AND A CRACKER SAVED RICKWOOD FIELD

Exactly five weeks after what all believed to be the final Barons game ever at Rickwood Field, the lights were turned on at another old Southern minor league ballpark. Durham Athletic Park—home of the Single-A Durham Bulls of the Carolina League—was alive with the sounds and the sights of small-town baseball. But it was all make-believe: the forty-seven-year-old ballpark was serving as a movie set. And the movie that was filmed in North Carolina that October, in the cool fall after Rickwood's seeming final summer, was a splendid film that captured the essence of baseball's minor leagues—*Bull Durham.*

Bull Durham's writer/director was Ron Shelton, a highly regarded, successful movie screenwriter. The film project he had won the right to direct in Durham was his first outing with creative control.

Shelton's entire life experience prepared him to make this picture. He'd played in the Orioles' minor league system in the 1960s and early 1970s. He was a good one, too. In his final season, he hit .260 as a middle infielder in Triple-A ball. But one of his teammates in the minors was future All-Star second baseman Bobby Grich, and Ron knew that the Baltimore organization—loaded with talent at every level (the Orioles won pennants in '66, '69, '70, '71, '79, and '83 and the World Series in '66, '70, and '83)—would be a tough place to make it all the way to the Show. So Ron Shelton retired at twenty-five and performed his second act in Hollywood.

The movie was, of course, an enormous hit, often regarded as a true classic sports film. Star Kevin Costner established himself as the go-to actor for baseball movies (he would star in another classic, *Field of Dreams,* filmed less than a year after *Bull Durham*) and newcomer Tim Robbins became a star (despite being thoroughly unconvincing as a pitcher). And Ron Shelton became a major player in Hollywood, a filmmaker who could get projects green-lighted simply by expressing his interest.

Shelton had another project, a film that he'd wanted to do for years. He wasn't a fan of typical sports movies such as *The Natural* in which the hero always homered in the bottom of the ninth or *Brian's Song* or *Pride of the Yankees* with a noble paragon dying in the final reel. Similar to what he had done in *Bull Durham,* Shelton wanted his narrative told from the ballplayer's point of view. And the story he wanted to tell was that of the brilliant, mercurial, difficult, and legendary Tyrus Raymond Cobb.

Ron wanted his Ty Cobb biographical film to be a character study. His narrative would focus on an elderly, long-retired Hall of Famer. Any baseball action included in the movie would be "flashback" sequences. The primary reason Shelton decided to keep the depiction of Cobb's legendary playing career to a minimum was rooted in realism: there just weren't any ballparks left in America in the 1990s that could pass for a stadium of the Georgia Peach's era. At least, that was what Ron Shelton thought.

And then, in 1993, Shelton heard about Rickwood Field, still standing—albeit precariously—in Birmingham, Alabama.

The Friends of Rickwood, a preservation group, had been brainstorming ideas in 1992, trying to come up with something—anything—that might save the doomed ballpark from looming demolition. Few options sprang to the imaginations of the five successful Birmingham businessmen—Coke Matthews, Tom Crosby, Terry Slaughter, Alan Farr, and Bill Cather—that gathered regularly to find a future for Rickwood. The five old friends spent many a happy day in their youth at ballgames at the already ancient field; now as adults, perhaps they were attempting to hold onto a part of their collective past that could not be saved. Every other old stadium of the great Southern Association and the greater Negro Leagues had fallen. Rickwood was in the bottom of the ninth, and the bench was empty.

And then, someone in the room remembered that only a couple of years earlier, Birmingham had turned down a request to film the movie *A League of Their Own* at Rickwood. Coke Matthews and Terry Slaughter were advertising men by profession. They realized that by using the ballpark as a filming venue for movies, they could get publicity for Rickwood that was both valuable and free—and film productions just might finance some desperately needed renovations.

That's how filmmaker Ron Shelton found himself on a private jet on loan from Alabama Governor Jim Folsom Jr.'s office in 1993, flying through dangerous storms into Birmingham. Ron later said that he had a fleeting thought about the last moments of Lynyrd Skynyrd, crashing on a similar Southern night two decades earlier. Perhaps Ron could hear "Sweet Home Alabama" in his head as the jet hurtled through the ominous clouds.

Fortunately for Ron Shelton, for Rickwood Field, and for baseball, the plane landed safely in Birmingham.

Ron was driven to the ballpark. It was still raining as it can only rain in the Deep South. Despite the best efforts of the Friends of Rickwood, the grandstand was in "horrific" condition, according to Coke Matthews. As Shelton stood on the diamond—the ball cap on his head drenched with the downpour—the gathered Friends of Rickwood steeled themselves for the certain disappointment of the big-time Hollywood director thanking them for their time before getting on the next available jet (after the weather cleared, of course) for LA.

But that wasn't what happened.

The talented moviemakers see things. Film is a visual art. And looking around Rickwood, Ron didn't see a crumbling edifice in a decaying neighborhood. He saw—to paraphrase another popular baseball-themed movie of the time—what had been good before and could be again. He clearly saw Rick Woodward's grandstand, he saw Connie Mack's diamond, he saw the greats of the game in flannel uniforms on a brilliant spring day.

"Let's do it," said Ron Shelton.

Warner Brothers allowed Ron a small budget for modest repairs to Rickwood. It was a godsend. By bringing the stadium up to filming standards, the most pressing concerns of the Friends of Rickwood were alleviated.

Filming began, and Birmingham's green cathedral was the site of a modern miracle. There was action and activity and even *excitement* in the West End. Cast as Ty Cobb, actor Tommy Lee Jones—who was awarded an Oscar for his role in *The Fugitive* as filming progressed—took the field in the uniform of the Detroit Tigers from before the Great War. As Cobb, he stared down a flannel-clad right-handed pitcher. Although the action was mock, the pitcher was real—played by seven-time Cy Young Award winner Roger Clemens. And in the venerable grandstand, playing a heckler without hands whom Cobb had attacked in a notorious incident, was Mobile-born singer/songwriter/bon vivant Jimmy Buffett (a personal friend of Shelton's, enlisted for a cameo).

Buffett had been a huge fan of the old Mobile Bears of the Southern Association and a regular at Hartwell Field, Mobile's old baseball park whose last remains were scuttled in 1983. At Rickwood, he actually played a special, spontaneous concert for the extras and the crew, standing atop one of the dugouts. For a moment, Mr. Mack met Margaritaville. The One Particular Harbour was an aged grandstand 275 miles from the Gulf.

There was life in Rickwood. Ron Shelton had given the field a fighter's chance. "(Shelton) was the angel sent to save Rickwood," said Coke Matthews.

Cobb was not a hit. It bombed. Too dark for audiences who wanted escapism at the movies, not enough baseball action for sports film enthusiasts. And in the years since release, the portrayal of Ty Cobb himself has drawn criticism—the Al Stump biography that Shelton used for source material has been called into serious question. Shelton knew Stump personally and trusted his version of events, but in the years since the author's death, there has been significant evidence that Stump—who despised Cobb—fabricated and/or embellished many of the negative events portrayed in his book and in the *Cobb* movie.

However, Ron Shelton's film was a smashing success for Rickwood Field. Now established as a prime location for period baseball movies, television productions, and even commercials, brisk activity at the stadium continues to the present day. Soon after *Cobb* wrapped, a remarkably realistic commercial for "Baby Ruth" candy bars was shot at Rickwood starring an actor who may have resembled the real Babe Ruth more than anyone who ever played him in any of his many film incarnations (with the possible exception of Ruth himself in *Pride of the Yankees*).

And full-scale film productions returned quickly—and often—to the West End after *Cobb.* In 1996, Home Box Office filmed *Soul of the Game*—an award-winning production about Satchel Paige, Josh Gibson, and Jackie Robinson, starring Blair Underwood, Mykelti Williamson, and Delroy Lindo—at the prime remaining Negro Leagues ballpark in America. Rickwood—the scene of more Negro Leagues history than any other stadium—was a fitting choice for a starring role.

And when *42*—a big-budget, major Hollywood retelling of Jackie Robinson's epic story starring major bankable stars Chadwick Boseman and Harrison Ford—was filmed in 2013, there was an obvious first choice as the primary action filming set: a place where Jackie Robinson played, both as a Negro Leaguer and as a Brooklyn Dodger. A place where, in 1954, Jackie and his Brooklyn Dodgers played the first integrated baseball game in Birmingham history.

Yes, Rickwood Field.

America's Oldest Ballpark was the primary filming location for the documentary *The League*, released in 2023. To pay homage to the Negro Leagues, director Sam Pollard artfully wove archival interviews with Willie Mays, Hank Aaron, Satchel Paige, and Buck O'Neil—all of whom played games at Rickwood—with footage from old Negro League games.

But it's the fictional movies—all make-believe, lights and shadows—that have been a very real, very concrete-and-steel part of saving Rickwood. And it all goes back to Ron Shelton and his vision.

Ron Shelton grew up in Southern California. His family was Baptist, and his father worked for an evangelical college. They were a very religious family, but Ron recalled—as an adult—one instance in which something came before their every-Sunday attendance at church.

The World Series of 1957 was on television, and the game conflicted with church services. But in 1957, the Milwaukee Braves were in the Series. And Eddie Mathews was the star third baseman of the Braves.

Eddie Mathews was from Ron Shelton's hometown. And Eddie was Ron's hero.

In the 10th inning of the fourth game of the 1957 World Series, the game Ron Shelton and his family skipped church (which they NEVER did) to watch, Eddie Mathews hit a walk-off two-run homer.

"We didn't go to church quite as much after that," said Ron.

But his lifelong love affair with the game had been escalated to a new level. Eddie Mathews and a walk-off homer to win the game (which, as a filmmaker, Ron Shelton claims to dislike as a plot point) has impacted his career to the present day.

Shelton almost certainly did not know it when he stood on the diamond at Rickwood in 1993, but Eddie Mathews had also stood on that diamond forty years before. The diamond Connie Mack had laid out more than forty years before that. The circular nature of the game displays itself: the players circle the bases and then return home.

Eddie Mathews did not play for the Birmingham Barons in the Southern Association. He played—and very, very well—for the Barons' most hated rivals, the Atlanta Crackers. And while with the Crackers, Mathews did something no one else ever managed to do in a regular league game in Southern Association history: he smashed a home run that actually hit the famous magnolia tree in

Ponce de Leon Park in Atlanta (a huge tree very deep in center field that was *in play*). And he hit it on the fly.

Ponce de Leon Park is long gone. In The Atlanta Way, it was bulldozed and obliterated several stadiums ago, without a second thought to memory or to legacy or to emotion.

But somehow, that tree—Eddie Mathews' tree—still stands where a ballpark used to be.

And Ron Shelton, who loved Eddie Mathews, helped make sure that another ballpark—the home of the Atlanta Crackers' greatest rivals—stands today.

And the guy who brought Ron Shelton and Rickwood together was named Matthews.

The script for *Bull Durham* was onto something. There really should be a Church of Baseball.

CHAPTER 21

ENDING A DECADE OF FRICTION

For 33 years, Curt Bloom was the radio voice of the Barons

Curt Bloom was the radio voice of the Birmingham Barons from 1992 through his retirement following the 2024 season. He had a prime seat and valuable perspective for the Rickwood Classic games held at Rickwood starting in 1996.

He recalled that when the Barons moved out of Rickwood and into Hoover Metropolitan Stadium in 1988, it created a lot of hard feelings on each side. "So much goes back to politics. I'm not proud of that, but it's the truth."

He explained that the ownership of the team asked the city of Birmingham for significant upgrades including more parking and better lighting. City leaders replied that they couldn't afford it. "It was definitely a war of words."

In the years following the team's move to Hoover, just south of Birmingham, bitterness festered between the Barons and the Magic City. "It was a decade of friction."

Bill Hardekopf was the team's GM. "He was my first boss, and I consider him my mentor," said Bloom. "He was the one, in my opinion, who had the idea to go back and play a game (at Rickwood). He wanted to mend the fences. He said, 'Let's do this turn-back-the-clock thing.'"

Also working for Hardekopf at the time was Jonathan Nelson, who rose through the ranks to become team president in 2013 before stepping down in 2025. He recalled his early years with the franchise starting in 1993, when he would call prospective customers for group outings at Barons games. "I called multiple people that still had resentment for the Barons moving from Rickwood to the Hoover Met. I'm like wow, that's lingering longer than expected. I learned that emotions run for a long time in Birmingham, Alabama."

The first Rickwood Classic, in which the Barons returned to Rickwood to play a regular-season game, was June 12, 1996. "It was one of the most satisfying events we ever held," Nelson said. "It was one of those magical days in which we turned back the clock and set in motion a tradition. It's beyond a special game."

"Since '96, the relationship between Rickwood and the Barons certainly improved," observed Bloom.

He didn't hesitate when asked which Classic game was the most memorable to him. "The first one, for sure." The Barons beat the Memphis Chicks that day, 3-2, in front of a capacity crowd of 10,334.

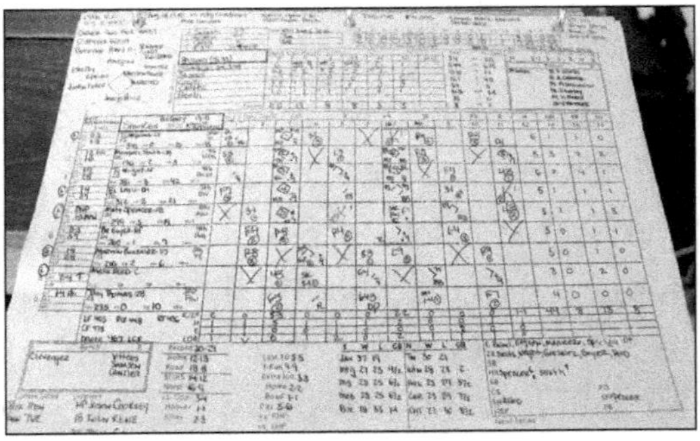

Bloom's meticulous scoresheets are archived in his old broadcast booth at Regions Field. This one is from the 2010 Rickwood Classic.

"You really can't say it a lot as a broadcaster, but I did have a favorite player. It was Mike Cameron, and he played in that game. He was one of four or five African-American players on the Barons at the time. I can still see Mike playing center field in that throwback uniform, playing where Willie Mays played. That was really an incredible moment."

Cameron went on to play for eight different major league teams, winning three Gold Gloves. His career highlight was hitting four home runs in a game for Seattle in 2002.

Joining Cameron in the starting lineup for the Barons in the 1996 contest were two other noteworthy names. Pete Rose Jr. went 2-for-3 while playing third base, and manning right field was Magglio Ordóñez, who went on to post an impressive 38.8 WAR (wins above replacement) over his fifteen years in the big leagues.

The deciding run that day was driven in by Ordóñez. "You just can't dream, you can't fathom something like that happening," said Bloom.

On one of his first on-location assignments for Minor League Baseball, Ben Hill interviewed Harmon Killebrew

The Classic on June 2, 2010, was special for numerous reasons, not the least of which was that it celebrated the 100th anniversary of the opening of Rickwood Field. The Barons invited Harmon Killebrew to attend and sign autographs for fans. Other former players invited over the years included Dale Murphy, Darryl Strawberry, and Dwight "Doc" Gooden, "but Harmon was in a league of his own," said Nelson. "He is in an elite tier of Hall of Famers to me. And he had played for Chattanooga at Rickwood back when they were a Twins farm team."

Nelson added that when he first approached Killebrew about appearing at the 2010 Classic, the retired slugger didn't haggle about the appearance fee whatsoever. "I just could not have been more impressed with him. He couldn't have been more gracious to our staff and to our fans."

Although the public didn't know it at the time, Killebrew had

This poster was used to promote the first Rickwood Classic, held in 1996

been diagnosed with cancer. He didn't let that stop him from keeping his commitment to appear. The baseball world mourned his passing the following May.

The Tennessee Smokies won the 2010 game, 8-7, in 11 innings. Covering it for Minor League Baseball was a young Benjamin Hill, in his second year of providing content for the minors' website. He went on to become the author of the popular newsletter *Ben's Biz Beat* (now called *The Baseball Traveler)*, as he reports on wacky promotions and intriguing ballparks. Many consider him MLB's unofficial ambassador for the minors.

He started making road trips on behalf of the minors in 2010. One of his first was to Birmingham. "I had become aware of the Rickwood Classic several years earlier and wanted to attend from the moment I heard about it," he explained.

"The ballpark lived up to my expectations, as it felt like a portal to another era. The vintage scoreboard, period advertisements, and old-school light towers made an immediate impression on me. I remember thinking that the game should have been sold out, that more people should know about this opportunity, to see a game in such a special ballpark like this."

Hill had recently covered the opening of the Hank Aaron Childhood Home and Museum in Mobile. There he met Willie Mays, Reggie Jackson, Bob Feller, Rickey Henderson ... and of course Hammerin' Hank. "Harmon Killebrew was before my time as a player, but of course I knew he was one of the greats. Coming off my stop to Mobile, I had yet another chance to interview a legend. I remember him as polite and accessible, eager to share stories from his days playing in Rickwood as a member of the Lookouts. I did not know he was sick at the time, I guess no one did, but when he passed, it made me extra grateful that I had had the opportunity to meet him."

At the Classic a year after the 100th Anniversary Celebration, Barons center fielder Justin Greene not only made a circus catch while crashing into the outfield wall, he won the game with a walk-off homer in the 11th inning. "I just wish it wasn't so hot," he said following the 98-degree afternoon.

A combination of COVID and Major League Baseball's usurping the governance of the minor leagues meant no Rickwood Classics from 2020 through 2023. Considering that these games represented the biggest single fundraising opportunity for the Friends of Rickwood each year, this stung. Fortunately, the touring baseball-sensation Savannah Bananas played games at Rickwood in 2022 and 2023, which helped plug the fundraising hole.

But with the arrival of MLB at Rickwood Field in 2024, the door was reopened for the Barons to return to the corner of 12th Street West and 2nd Avenue West. As part of MLB's three-day extravaganza, the Barons faced off against the Montgomery Biscuits on June 18. A crowd of 7,866 watched as Birmingham fell, 6-5. Future major leaguers Brooks Baldwin, Edgar Quero, Tim Elko, and Jairo Iriarte were in the Barons' starting lineup that day.

This was the first Barons game at Rickwood since the city of Birmingham and MLB combined to invest millions of dollars in Rickwood and the surrounding temporary facilities installed for the event.

The 2024 contest was also Bloom's last Classic as lead broadcaster. And he definitely felt a big difference between that game and all of the previous ones.

"I consider myself blessed beyond belief to have seen what Rickwood looked like before the changes. For the first twenty-plus years, (the Classic) had an authentic and legitimate minor league feel. Hey, if your equipment blows up, that's on you, man. But in 2024, I felt like I was in a big-league stadium. No matter what I needed, guys were coming out of the woodwork to fix whatever was wrong. That's because of all of the resources that MLB brought."

The most memorable moment of the 2024 Classic didn't have to do with the ballpark or the game itself. It was the evening that Birmingham's native son Willie Mays died. "At one point early in the game, my phone started blowing up with messages asking me if I'd heard about Willie," Bloom recalled. He waited until the Giants made an official announcement before he informed his listening audience.

"But there's another part of the story about that game. The Barons had come out flat and trailed by five runs after two innings. We were getting our butt kicked, plus it was so hot. But after there was a moment of silence for Willie, something happened. Through the power of the Say Hey Kid, we mounted an unbelievable rally. It was like his energy had passed through the bodies of the players. In the bottom of the ninth, we had the potential winning run in scoring position, but we couldn't pull off the miracle."

Bloom started a full-circle moment during the 2014 Classic, when the Mississippi Braves beat the Barons, 5-4. Longtime minor league broadcaster Doug Greenwald had come to Rickwood on an off day for his Fresno Grizzlies. "If you've been a broadcaster in Minor League Baseball for at least five years, you know Doug's name. Because of everything he's done in baseball, I had him join me on the air. I knew he'd appreciate doing a game at Rickwood more than anybody else that drives this highway."

When Bloom retired after the 2024 season, he recommended Greenwald to Barons management. For the 2025 season, Doug was the voice of the Barons, which meant he was behind the mic for that year's Rickwood Classic. Whom did he invite to join him on the air? Curt Bloom, thus completing the full-circle moment.

The 2025 Classic, a 1-0 Barons loss to the Rocket City Trash Pandas, was played in front of 4,190 fans on June 4.

"No matter in what capacity you're there, it's a thrill," said Greenwald following his broadcast. "Rickwood is a magnet for fans who got their first taste of baseball there, passing it on to the next generation and seeing the ones who years from now will share the same experience. It's amazing how a 115-year-old structure is meant for the kid in all of us—it makes Birmingham the 'Magic' attraction every year. And returning the favor of having Curt on the broadcast added to the magic for me."

In much the way Killebrew delighted fans who attended the 2010 Classic, Hall of Fame pitcher Jim Kaat appeared in 2025. "We had realized that having a celebrity guest was one of the biggest pieces of the Rickwood Classic recipe," noted Nelson. "We're thrilled we had Jim Kaat here."

Hall of Famer Jim Kaat greeted fans and signed autographs at the 2025 Rickwood Classic

The lefthander with stunning longevity also had an illustrious career in the broadcast booth, earning seven Emmys. Kaat spoke at a breakfast at Regions Field before attending the game at Rickwood that afternoon. He explained that he'd pitched at Rickwood in 1959 when he was with the Lookouts. Both at Chattanooga's Engel Stadium and at Rickwood, "they had 'colored-only' stands and bathrooms back then. As a Midwest kid, I'd never seen that before. I still have guilt feelings for when our team bus had to stop and pick up (our Black players) at a different hotel than ours."

As the 2025 game was being played, bulldozers were working on replacing the playing surface at Willie Mays Park, the youth baseball field less than five miles from Rickwood in Mays' boyhood neighborhood of Fairfield. This fulfilled a promise made by MLB when it announced the 2024 event.

"We never saw our time there (MLB at Rickwood Field in 2024) as

MLB kept its promise of renovating Willie Mays Park in Fairfield

a one-time engagement for our sport," said MLB's senior VP of social responsibility April Brown. "That's why we're excited to have this current opportunity right in front of us right now. Right in the town where the great Willie Mays grew up, at a field that was named in his honor in 1985. A field that—after a few decades of wear and tear and use—could use a little love."

Two weeks later, on the Juneteenth holiday, MLB hosted another event at Rickwood to honor the Negro Leagues. Dubbed the East West Classic, the same name attached to the Negro League All-Star Games eight and nine decades earlier, it featured former big leaguers playing a lighthearted game on Rickwood's hallowed turf. Participants included 2025 Hall of Fame inductee C.C. Sabathia and Bloom's favorite player, Mike Cameron.

All told, the Barons have participated in twenty-six Rickwood Classics through 2025, with the most frequent opponent being the Chattanooga Lookouts, who've made the trek down I-59 seven times. The Barons' record in Classic games is 11-15, with 6,553 being the average crowd.

David Kronheim, nicknamed the Number Tamer, compiles the most comprehensive analyses of big-league and minor league attendance figures. He calculates that during the seasons when the Barons played a Rickwood Classic game, their average home crowd has been 4,649—or 1,904 less than at the Classics. More proof that fans love these contests at America's Oldest Ballpark.

Nelson said the logistics of playing a game at Rickwood each year are "a heavy lift for us, yet at the same time, it's a labor of love.

I know when the dust settles on the final out, the fans always enjoy it."

He added that, "Everyone who participates in the games—umpires, staff, visiting celebrities, opposing players, the Barons players—invariably say, 'Why don't we do this more?' They all recognize how cool and fun it is. They all say what an honor it is to be a part of such a game."

Until MLB decreed that the dugouts had to be enlarged for the 2024 big-league game, players routinely sat on the dugout roof, like at this 2010 game

CHAPTER 22

SWEARING ON MY MOTHER'S GRAVE

With a history dating to 1876 when the National League was formed, big-league ball had experienced it all—the dead-ball era, the formation of the Hall of Fame (based on dubious claims that the sport was invented in Cooperstown, New York), bigger-than-life legends, West Coast baseball, scandals, strikes, and a juiced baseball (and perhaps some juiced players) that prompted skyrocketing home run numbers. The sport had truly seen everything.

MLB headquarters in Manhattan showed that it still had some tricks up its sleeves, though. Based on the dual desires of creating unique experiences for fans and bringing the sport to places it had never been, MLB execs starting brainstorming ideas for out-of-the-ordinary "jewel" events in 2014.

Baseball appeals to patriotism perhaps more than any other sport, so the first possible endeavor involved bringing a big-league game to a military base. MLB sent a team of experts to Fort Bragg, North Carolina, in 2015 to assess the feasibility of holding a regular-season game there. As there was no facility suitable to host such a major event, MLB built its own. It focused on an abandoned golf course on the base that was flat enough for a temporary ballpark to be constructed. The phrase "pop-up ballpark" originated with this project, as something resembling an erector set accommodated enough bleachers so that 12,500 military personnel and their families could enjoy a night of baseball.

On July 3, 2016, the Miami Marlins defeated their division rival Atlanta Braves, 5-2, at Fort Bragg Field. Numerous boxes were checked by the event, providing ESPN with a compelling Sunday Night Baseball matchup on the eve of the Fourth of July. Said MLB

Chief Operating Officer Tony Petitti, "Our primary goals were to extend gratitude to our service members, to let them enjoy the first major league game ever in North Carolina, and to leave behind a recreational facility as a legacy for the event."

Just as importantly, it provided "proof of concept" that this type of one-off game could succeed logistically and thematically, and that it could fascinate fans across the country.

What followed was a series of such "jewel" regular-season contests, each more popular and elaborate than the last: at the Little League World Series in 2017; in San Juan, Puerto Rico, in 2018; at the College World Series stadium in Omaha and at London Stadium in England in 2019; and at the *Field of Dreams* movie site in Dyersville, Iowa, in 2021 and 2022.

Meanwhile, Gerald Watkins had ascended to the position of executive director of the Friends of Rickwood, having added the title to his post as the group's chairman of the board. "I had a great imagination for baseball," he recalled. "I thought, 'What can I do to make Rickwood better?'"

In the spring of 2021, he reached out to Major League Baseball to see if there was interest in playing a game at Rickwood. It took about six months for a formal response, but league leaders took Watkins' suggestion seriously.

"They made me swear on my mother's grave I wouldn't talk about it," Watkins laughed. "They were really firm about that. They told me that if I told anybody, and it gets back to your mayor and your governor, they will pester the hell out of us. And we don't operate under that kind of pressure."

According to Watkins, MLB then added: "Don't call us. We'll call you."

In February 2022, MLB contacted Watkins to confirm its interest in staging an event at Rickwood. MLB's next overture to Watkins was during the All-Star break that summer, which led to an October visit by the same advance team utilized at all of the sport's previous jewel events. In addition to representatives from MLB headquarters, the group included Populous (architecture and event planning), BaAM (construction and logistics management), and BrightView (playing surface and ballpark structures).

The team of experts snapped photos, made drawings, and took measurements. "A couple of months later, they came back with diagrams and schemes," said Watkins. "They said they were ready to move forward, and the estimated cost was $2.5 million."

Note that this wasn't what MLB was spending. This is what Birmingham and the Friends of Rickwood were expected to spend on improvements to the ballpark. To be fair, MLB intended to pay the costs of actually staging the event: erecting a tent city for players and the media and providing concession stands, port-a-potties, temporary light towers, and staffing. While MLB doesn't disclose such costs, the total surely ran into the millions of dollars.

Funding for a new playing surface, the replacement of dugouts, padding on the walls, netting, numerous repairs, and making the 114-year-old facility compliant for those with disabilities was all to come from "local sources," as Watkins put it.

The Friends of Rickwood started raising money. When they had accumulated about $800,000 in pledges, a new bombshell hit. "That's when we learned that the estimated cost had gone up to $5 million."

Faced with such a steep path, many municipalities would've thrown in the towel and told MLB it can play someplace else.

Not Birmingham.

Chaz Mitchell, chief operating officer for the city of Birmingham, was involved in all discussions with MLB on the possibility of hosting a big-league game. "We knew that the investment had to be pretty substantial in order to have this MLB-regulated stadium for their multimillion-dollar players to feel safe.

"We were saying that if we make this investment, we know that we're not doing it for just one game. We're doing it for the future of Rickwood and all it can do."

Mitchell added that he told MLB that if the city provided the funding, MLB needed to be "willing to let us hire a local minority firm within the city of Birmingham to help with the renovations."

As a result, AG Gaston Construction of Birmingham was brought in to help with the work on Rickwood.

The city stepped up to fund $5.5 million. Mitchell said that this didn't divert funding from other needs, because the city budget had a surplus that year. Not only that, "We were told we could take the money we'd already raised and put it in the bank for (future) maintenance and upkeep," explained Watkins.

In June 2023, MLB finally announced to the public that it intended to honor the Negro Leagues by bringing a three-day event to Rickwood Field a year later, with the centerpiece being a regular-season game between the San Francisco Giants and St. Louis Cardinals. The date would be June 20, 2024.

But there was much work to do to prepare America's Oldest Ballpark for this once-in-a-lifetime event.

CHAPTER 23

ENSURING THE LEGACY

Murray Cook, president of BrightView's Sports Turf Division, was part of the advance team that MLB brought to assess Rickwood Field in 2022. He'd been acting as MLB's chief ballpark consultant since 1993, when he traveled to London to prepare a cricket stadium for a Minor League Baseball game.

This was his first visit to Rickwood. "In looking at the wooden ballpark, it brought back memories of some of the old stadiums I worked in over the years," he recalled. "It gave me that feeling of a really unique, cool place. You could tell it had a lot of stories."

Then reality started to set in. He noticed the mammoth distance from home plate to the backstop, the difference between the wooden outfield fence and the imposing concrete walls beyond, and the irregular foul poles.

And then there was the playing surface, Cook's lifelong area of expertise. "The field was basically a rec-level field. It was in really poor condition. It had been rented out for everything, so you could tell it had been loved a lot. The bump running down the middle of the field was so high that if you were in the (first-base) dugout and your left fielder was shorter than five feet, you wouldn't be able to see him at all."

Normally, Cook could look at a natural playing surface and identify the type of grass. "What was there? I couldn't tell you. We used to call that '3-you grass.' It's you, you, and you, because you're not sure what it is. Some weeds, some grass, some Bermuda, some more weeds.

"Then we walked down and looked at the foul lines. They'd been putting chalk down the foul line for, I don't know, 100 years or so.

In 1993, Rickwwod was officially added to the National Register of Historic Places, which limits changes that can be made.

That line was literally a foot higher than the field on either side of it. When we eventually took out the foul line, there was almost eight inches of white chalk that had built up over the years.

"So we knew right away the field had to be completely replaced."

The BrightView crews removed the top two feet of the existing surface, then installed a complete drainage system as if this were a new major league ballpark being constructed. That system can drain up to ten inches of water per hour. Then gravel was spread out, a sand mixture to act as a root zone, and finally the sod (Tahoma 31 Bermudagrass for those of you keeping score at home).

BrightView was also responsible for replacing the dugouts (the old ones were "like bunkers" said Cook), some of the fencing, and the foul poles, as well as installing netting all around the foul territory.

"The biggest challenge we had was that we wanted to ensure we maintained the magic of the venue, its history, what had been there so long, to ensure the legacy is taken care of. This is very different than when you have a clean slate to work with."

Todd Barnes, senior VP of event planning for sports architecture giant Populous, agrees. In addition to managing Super Bowls and other mega-sporting events, he's been part of the advance teams working on MLB's jewel events going back to Fort Bragg in 2016. "The difference between Rickwood and, say, Fort Bragg or Field of Dreams is that we basically had a blank slate to work with in those other places. At Rickwood, we were handed a stadium that we had to make function for us."

In addition to creating spaces for clubhouses, concessions, a fan plaza, and more, the necessary renovations to the existing ballpark had to be taken into account. "We had to decide the architectural needs of this ballpark that is 100 years old, because it had to transcend to the current century and the current decade."

No easy task.

A major obstacle was making Rickwood wheelchair-accessible, which was an enormous concern since many of the surviving Negro League players were arriving in wheelchairs. Hindering this was the limited number of portals for fans to enter the seating bowl from the exterior, and the steepness of their ramps.

Because of the cramped quarters underneath the stands, Populous decided to forgo the use of existing restrooms or concession stands. Instead, dozens of port-a-potties and temporary concession points of sale were part of the "tent city" erected in the flat field just across 2nd Avenue, which is usually used for parking. Interestingly, much of the dirt removed when the field was excavated was spread across this space, eliminating another problem of where to dump it.

All of this fan plaza was within a new outer perimeter fence used just for this three-day event. And that perimeter was adjacent to many homes in the neighborhood—some occupied, others vacant. "This was such a tight site overall, and getting the adjacency relationships of functional elements to be able to flow together in the right way made the event day a success."

Another consideration is that Rickwood is on the National Register of Historic Places, meaning some renovations were off-limits. For instance, most of the concrete stairs in the seats are uneven, but the whole under-structure of the seating bowl couldn't be ripped out and replaced. "Fortunately, we were able to make modifications that were necessary to play a Major League Baseball game there," noted Barnes. As for the treacherous stairs, extra ushers were positioned to keep patrons from falling or tripping.

In addition to BrightView and Populous, BaAM is another key member of MLB's jewel-event team. It was responsible for building the temporary structures needed for the event, and it worked with MLB to create the right look and feel of the structures and to avoid any bottlenecks in the traffic flow of fans.

The vendor hired to coordinate parking (since there was practically none on-site) was SP+. Most attendees felt the aspect of having fans park at nearby Legion Field and taking shuttle buses to Rickwood worked smoothly. A subcontractor that BaAM utilized for installing the plumbing and fixtures in the temporary structures was Sanitrax. Using them "was a real game-changer," according to Barnes.

"There is a lot of thought and perspective, and a lot of Zoom meetings that go into all the development of the plans," he added. "Major League Baseball has looked at their vendors in a way that we provide equal expertise in each of our own areas, but we have been continuing with them for many years so that we really understand in a great way how each other works."

Of course, numerous departments within MLB headquarters worked on the planning as well. The Global Events folks "oversee the event experience and presentation in the ballpark at our jewel events," said MLB vice president Brian O'Gara. His department, headed by senior VP Jeremiah Yolkut, started working on the entertainment surrounding the event before it had even been announced to the public.

"We were very mindful that the entire show should feel like a blend of today's game and the aura and atmosphere that Rickwood Field represented historically," O'Gara explained.

With all of that planning and preparation behind them, those who had worked so feverishly for this moment were ready to hold the biggest baseball event in Alabama's history.

CHAPTER 24

SEA LIONS AND STARS

> *Major League Baseball today announced that* ***Rickwood Field****, the oldest professional ballpark in the United States and former home of the Birmingham Black Barons of the Negro Leagues, will be the site of a special Regular Season contest between the St. Louis Cardinals and San Francisco Giants on June 20, 2024.*

Thus began the press release from Major League Baseball on June 20, 2023, exactly one year before it was to stage a regular-season game at America's Oldest Ballpark.

In the years leading up to this, MLB had been embracing the legacy of the Negro Leagues after largely ignoring it for decades. In December 2020, MLB announced that henceforth it would consider the players in seven Negro Leagues from 1920 through 1948 to be major leaguers, and that their stats would be incorporated into the history of the big leagues.

Following three years of research, in May 2024, MLB announced that the individual stats of 2,300 players had officially been accounted for and had been folded into the historical record. The problem, though, was that box scores and official accounts from Negro League games were hard to come by, and only batting and pitching stats from reliable sources were included.

This meant, for instance, that no home runs were added to Willie Mays' official lifetime total. Newspaper articles reported home runs, but no box scores could be located, so his career total remained at 660.

The inclusion of these statistics occurred a month before MLB brought its extravaganza to Rickwood. Following the somewhat inauspicious results of MLB's three years of research, the events in Birmingham in June 2024 were the most tangible way the big leagues could honor the Negro Leagues.

It's obvious that MLB and its team of vendors greatly expanded the experience for fans at its jewel events from Fort Bragg in 2016 to Rickwood in 2024. The original event at the Army base basically consisted of the game itself. At the Little League World Series, the MLB players spent the afternoon with the Little Leaguers. At the Field of Dreams, they added a minor league game two days prior to the big-league contest—plus, in Year Two they added a postgame concert by country artist Walker Hayes, which greatly aided in spreading out the traffic flow that night.

For the 2024 MLB Rickwood Field event, they pulled out all of the stops.

Since the proceedings were to honor the Negro Leagues, it was all timed to occur around the Juneteenth holiday, which became a federal holiday in the U.S. in 2021.

The first day of events was Tuesday, June 18. In the afternoon, MLB hosted a showing of the HBO documentary *Say Hey Willie Mays* at the Carver Theater in Birmingham.

That evening, the hometown Birmingham Barons, wearing throwback uniforms of the Black Barons, played a regular-season game against the Montgomery Biscuits, playing as the Gray Sox. It was the first "Rickwood Classic" since 2019. Interestingly, it

Mays' uniform number of 24 was very prominent on the field

was the Biscuits that gave up the home game to participate in this matchup, as the two teams resumed their six-game series in Montgomery the following evening.

This minor league game at Rickwood, the Barons' home for decades before moving to Hoover in 1988, drew a huge crowd of 7,866, more than double the team's average of 3,608 at Regions Field, their current home, that season.

And every one of those fans in attendance will remember the PA announcement made following the seventh inning:

> *The San Francisco Giants, Major League Baseball and the Willie Mays family announce that the Say Hey Kid, Willie Mays, one of the greatest players in the history of our game, has passed away at the age of ninety-three. He was born here in Alabama and got his start in this very ballpark, thrilled generations of baseball fans with his brilliant play, and we will always cherish the memory and life of the great Willie Mays.*

The stunned crowd was silent for a moment. Suddenly, a handful of fans started clapping. More rose to their feet and applauded, and soon the largest ovation of the evening was being served up to the heavens, where the crowd was sure the Say Hey Kid was smiling down on them. A chant of "Willie! Willie! Willie!" filled the 114-year-old ballpark where he had patrolled center field as a sixteen-year-old.

Even though seven innings had already been played, this was the emotional beginning of MLB's three-day event. A video tribute to Mays was then played on the temporary video board in right field.

The story behind the announcement to the crowd is fascinating. When word reached MLB's production center at Rickwood that Mays had just passed away, Brian O'Gara was next to the public address announcer. He grabbed his phone and started writing the script to be read to the crowd. "While we were determining when and how we and MLB Network were going to acknowledge (Mays' passing), I was writing on my phone, knowing that this crowd in the ballpark, where this legend got his start, did not have this information.

"Of course, the crowd response after the announcement was so heartwarming that all of us will remember that," he said. And months after witnessing that scene, "I still have chills thinking about it."

The hometown Barons lost a tight game to the Biscuits that night, 6-5, but MLB's whirlwind in the Magic City was underway.

The jam-packed schedule continued the following day—the actual Juneteenth holiday—with the MLB Diversity Pipeline Program Workshop. MLB said this event was for "underrepresented talent in sports medicine, including athletic trainers, physical therapists, and students interested in biomechanics and performance science."

That afternoon, a mural of Mays by artist Chuck Styles was dedicated on the side of a building at the corner of 1st Street and 18th Street in downtown Birmingham.

Birmingham Mayor Randall Woodfin spoke at the dedication ceremony for the Willie Mays mural.

That evening back at Rickwood was the Barnstorm Birmingham Celebrity Softball Game. Ruben Studdard, Birmingham native and *American Idol* winner, sang the national anthem. Mays' godson Barry Bonds and Hall of Famer Derek Jeter were the honorary team captains. Players included former big leaguers, entertainers and local celebrities.

The cornerstone event was the following day, on June 20. The St. Louis Cardinals, playing as the Negro League Stars, faced the San Francisco Giants, playing as the Sea Lions, which was the city's entry in the West Coast Negro League in the 1940s. Many major leaguers had played barnstorming games at Rickwood, and the field had hosted many major league exhibitions, but this marked the first time a regular-season game had been held in the state of Alabama.

The MLB Network and Fox both aired pregame shows. One portion of the Fox banter went viral. Alex Rodriguez asked Reggie Jackson, who had played for the Birmingham A's in 1967, "How emotional is it for you to come back?" Here is part of Jackson's response:

> *Coming back here is not easy. The racism when I played here, the difficulty of going through different places where we traveled. Fortunately, I had a manager and I had players on the team that helped me get through it. But I wouldn't wish it on anybody. People said to me today, I spoke, and they said, "Do you think you're a better person, do you think you won when you played here and conquered?" I said, "You know, I would never want to do it again." I walked into restaurants, and they would point at me and say, "The nigger can't eat here." I would go to a hotel, and they'd say, "The nigger can't stay here." We went to Charlie Finley's country club for a welcome home dinner, and they pointed me out with the n-word, "He can't come in here." Finley marched the whole team out. Finally, they let me in there, and he said, "We're going to go to the diner and eat hamburgers. We'll go where we're wanted." Fortunately, I had a manager in Johnny McNamara that, if I couldn't eat in a place, nobody would eat. We'd get food to travel. If I couldn't stay in a hotel, they'd drive*

> *to the next hotel and find a place where I could stay. Had it not been for Rollie Fingers, Johnny McNamara, Dave Duncan, Joe and Sharon Rudi—I slept on their couch three, four nights a week for about a month and a half. Finally, they were threatened that they would burn our apartment complex down unless I got out ... I wouldn't wish it on anyone. At the same time, had it not been for my white friends, had it not been for a white manager, and Rudi, Fingers, and Duncan, and Lee Meyers, I would have never made it.*

Those comments have been viewed online hundreds of thousands of times.

The fact that the theme of the event was to honor Negro Leaguers was not lost on the Cardinals and Giants players and coaches.

In noting that too few Blacks choose baseball as their chosen sport to play, Cardinals shortstop Masyn Winn told reporters: "It's our job to go out there and show these kids that it's fun to be out there and play baseball and compete at the highest level. ... It's hard not to love the game."

After spending the day attending the events sponsored by MLB in Birmingham, Cards manager Oliver Marmol said: "This game is going to be awesome, but getting involved with the community is even better. I just wish we had an off-day here to actually do more in the community prior to leaving."

The capacity for the game was 8,300. About a fourth of the seats were donated to community and youth organizations in Birmingham. Also, all 157 living Negro League players were invited, and about sixty of them were able to attend—most in wheelchairs or walking with canes.

Watching the parade of wheelchairs go by on their way to the field for pregame introductions, Negro Leagues Baseball Museum president Bob Kendrick remarked: "I remained always hopeful that this day would come. Any of us charged with being the stewards of the history of the Negro Leagues can't help but feel a sense of pride about this.

"I once asked the great Buck O'Neil why it was so important to

Bob Kendrick, President of the Negro League Baseball Museum, was "so proud" that MLB honored the Negro Leagues

him for there to be a Negro Leagues Museum. He told me, 'So we would be remembered.' I think Buck couldn't have imagined something like this happening.

"So proud. So proud," he concluded.

BaseballParks.com reported that Jake Flynn, a Giants fan living in Los Angeles, crossed the country with his fiancée Emily Kurbin to attend the events at Rickwood. But it wasn't just to see his favorite team play.

"Both of my parents were raised in the Bay area," he said, "so I grew up going to Candlestick Park and Pac Bell." What drew him to Alabama, though, was what he called "a once-in-a-lifetime opportunity."

"The second I heard it was going to happen, I didn't feel I had a choice," Flynn said. "I had to come."

He's glad he did. "It's hard not being emotional walking around here."

Adding to the vintage feel was a refurbished hand-operated scoreboard in left field. On top was a face clock, but its hands never moved. That's because it was permanently set to 8:24. You see, Mays wore number 8 with the Black Barons and 24 with the Giants. An excellent—and subtle—tribute.

MLB put a lot of thought into all aspects of the game. The umpires that day—Alan Porter, Adrian Johnson, Malachi Moore and C.B. Bucknor—are Black, as is Jeremiah Paprocki, the PA announcer. Paprocki, who normally does the PA for Cubs games at Wrigley

Field, "has a terrific voice, and is also sort of an old soul when it comes to baseball," noted O'Gara.

"For these jewel-event games, we get people from a variety of teams. We look at it as showcasing the best of MLB."

And speaking of showcases, the musical entertainment prior to the game rivaled that of a Super Bowl halftime show. Seven-time Grammy winner Jon Batiste sang, played piano, and danced across the infield of Rickwood amid dancers evoking the Jazz Era, when the Negro Leagues were at their peak. It was a dazzling display of preparation and talent.

Give the credit to MLB's Global Events team.

Back in 2023, O'Gara and senior manager Caylor Escalante were brainstorming on "how to build a pregame ceremony that captured the vibrancy and essence of our celebration of the Negro Leagues with a musical component. Instantly, Jon Batiste came to mind for Caylor. When we approached his camp, he was all-in, and he inspired everyone even more by his enthusiasm for the project," recalled O'Gara.

Escalante worked closely with Batiste's collaborator Jemel McWilliams on planning the music and choreography for the Birmingham event. On the night of the game, as the music played and the dancers danced, the Negro Leaguers were brought onto the field, escorted by the Cardinals and Giants players. "It felt like a culmination of the story that Jon was representing musically.

The Cardinals and Giants stood behind the Negro League players as Jon Batiste performed on the field

"It was magic."

Fox's portrayal of it all for the viewing audience never missed a beat. O'Gara credited the

Fox's broadcast team of Joe Davis and John Smoltz did the play by play from the gondola atop Rickwood's roof.

network's director Matt Gangl for coordinating it so precisely.

Handling the game's play-by-play duties for Fox were Joe Davis and John Smoltz. Their broadcast "booth" was actually the gondola perched on Rickwood's roof, directly behind home plate. The telecast even produced a half inning in black-and-white with low-resolution audio to evoke a vintage feel.

Throughout it all, there was a recurring tribute to the recently passed Mays.

For all the special touches, Fox's broadcast was awarded a Sports Emmy for *Outstanding Live Special.* Davis, meanwhile, won the Emmy for *Outstanding Personality–Play By Play.*

Moments before the game, Willie Mays' son Michael—flanked by Barry Bonds and Ken Griffey Jr.—addressed the crowd. Instead of the expected moment of silence, he said the crowd should participate in a moment of celebration, since his father was watching from above. O'Gara pointed out, "It was really impactful that the son of a legend had that insight to say that this is what we should do."

It was a very moving moment.

The Rev. Bill Greason then tossed the ceremonial first pitch. He was a brilliant choice for the honor, as he was a Marine in combat in World War II, a starting pitcher for the Black Barons in the 1940s (and teammate of Mays), the first Black player on the Cardinals, and for the previous fifty-four years, the senior pastor at Bethel Baptist Church, less than two miles from Rickwood Field. He celebrated his 100th birthday three months after the MLB event.

And, oh yes, there was the game itself.

Andre Pallante was the starting pitcher for St. Louis that evening. He was credited with the win in the 6-5 Cardinals victory. Brendan Donovan, who grew up in Enterprise, Alabama, was the hitting star, going 3-for-4 with a double and home run.

The most poignant aspect of the game is that both homers, one by the Giants' Heliot Ramos and the other by Donovan, sailed over the fence in right field. This is exactly where the "colored only" section—which had practically the only seats in the stadium without a roof overhead to block the sun—was located during the days of segregation.

An article in *USA TODAY* about the game pointed out that "those bleachers are gone, as is segregation. But the lessons of that time need to be remembered. That's why this game honoring the Negro Leagues shouldn't be a one-off occurrence. Now that there is a brand-new multimillion-dollar playing surface and the heavy lifting of figuring how to pull this off has been perfected, it's time to make this an annual event."

CHAPTER 25

FATHERS AND SONS ... AND GRANDSONS

"The diamond encloses what we are," said Donald Hall in an essay in *Fathers Playing Catch With Sons,* and so it does. Perhaps more than at any other single site, what Birmingham was—and what Birmingham is—can be glimpsed today at Rickwood Field.

Look at the fine old grandstand, largely untouched by the 2024 renovations for MLB, and you will see the pride and prosperity of a young Birmingham in 1910. Look at the reconstructed, hand-operated scoreboard and you will understand the competition between Southern cities in the era of high hopes right after the Second World War. And look to distant right field, where the "colored-only" bleachers once stood, and you will sense the distance that Birmingham had to travel to put Jim Crow behind it.

From the ballpark's beginnings early in the last century, as Birmingham's ironworks were making way for steel foundries, the process of forging legendary ballplayers started. A well-deserved plaque in the Alabama Sports Hall of Fame honors Rick Woodward, the industrialist who intensely loved the sport of baseball. So much so that he built Rickwood Field for the princely sum of $75,000, an unheard-of amount at the time.

As the plaque attests, "During Woodward's ownership, the Barons reportedly sent more players to the Majors than any other team." Add to that the number of Negro Leaguers who played at Rickwood and were never allowed to play in "white" baseball, plus the ones who came along in the 1940s and '50s who were given the chance, and you have a stunning list ... from Satch to the Diz, Benny and Willie, Piper and Pie, and the Moose from Moosup.

In all, 182 members of the National Baseball Hall of Fame have appeared at Rickwood, an amazing 61% of the players and managers enshrined in Cooperstown.

As MLB and the Fox TV Network told the world in 2024, Rickwood Field's place in sports history is undeniable, even if it took far too long for the sport to recognize it ... and to recognize the pivotal place occupied by the Negro Leagues and its players.

But what is the future for a structure that's over a century old?

"We were very, very thankful for MLB to sit at the table with me and the Friends of Rickwood at the beginning to figure out how not just to do renovations for one game, but for a lifetime to salute everything that has gone on in that stadium," explained Birmingham chief operating officer Chaz Mitchell.

"It is a historic, living, breathing stadium that you can't just ignore. You have to take care of it and make sure that the legacy lives on. We're thankful for MLB lighting a fire under us that we needed to take care of something that is a significant landmark in Birmingham."

And not just Birmingham. For the entire sport of baseball.

After the city invested $5.5 million on numerous improvements at Rickwood—not the least of which is a major league playing surface—the ballpark stands ready to host even more events. Mitchell believes that the facility should be in a "rotation" for regular-season games in the big leagues.

"I think we have that relationship with MLB," Mitchell explained. "They now know that we are able to put the investment towards renovations and upkeep. It'll be in the city's interest and for, I think, MLB to continue this and not let it be a one-off thing, but something that can be a staple event for MLB, whether it be yearly or biennial or whatever."

When the St. Louis Cardinals came to town in June 2024, manager Oli Marmol was asked by a reporter if he thought that there should be more big-league games at Rickwood. "Yeah, I actually talked to (commissioner Rob) Manfred about that this morning, about coming back and having other teams get to experience it. It's really cool not only for the city, but for the players and staff to get to experience this, so I would definitely welcome that."

As would baseball fans from coast to coast.

In the introduction of this book, we related a story about a Birmingham man who admired Stan Musial, and how the power of his passion was passed down to his son, and ultimately to the grandson he never knew. We held that the history of Rickwood is ultimately about fathers and sons, and so it is. In so many ways.

Oscar W. Adams Sr. was a prominent Black businessman in the segregated Birmingham of the 1920s. He owned the Black Barons when the team's star was the immortal Satchel Paige. But the successful Mr. Adams was largely unknown to white baseball fans who attended "real" Barons games at Rickwood. However, when the Barons left Rickwood to move to Hoover in 1987, Adams' son Oscar W. Adams Jr. was familiar to a large number of Alabamians, regardless of race.

He was a judge sitting on the Supreme Court of Alabama, the first Black man ever elected to statewide office. It is certainly a long way from the right-field bleachers at Rickwood Field to the highest government circles of the state, but it is a trip that the Adams family and Birmingham made in a single generation.

The owner of the other Barons that played at Rickwood also had sons.

Rick Woodward named his first son after his father Joseph. He named his second son after himself. Rick Jr., who died in 1987, also had a son to whom the family name of Alan Harvey Woodward III—and the persistent nickname of Rick—naturally descended. A second son was Robert, who goes by Bob.

And with Rick Woodward III and his brother Bob, another family circle formed around the West End diamond their grandfather built in 1910. When a group of civic leaders and old-fashioned baseball fans organized in 1992 to save and restore ancient Rickwood—by then recognized as the oldest baseball park in America—familiar Birmingham names took an active role in the restoration efforts.

However, while the first Rick Woodward helped plan a new ballpark to show what Birmingham could be, Rick III and Bob, along with other dedicated "friends of Rickwood," worked to save the old ballpark to show the nation that Birmingham has not forgotten how good it has been ... and will be. And because it was spared the wrecking ball in the 1990s when its future was decidedly in doubt, it was still standing for MLB to use as a vehicle for its long-overdue recognition of Negro League baseball in 2024.

Gerald Watkins, executive director of the Friends of Rickwood

The grandsons were quite visible at the big-league game, and again at the Rickwood Classic in 2025. At the latter, Bob noted that his great-grandfather and grandfather loved the city of Birmingham, and his granddad adored the sport of baseball. The Woodward descendants, he said, "are very proud to be a part of this city and in maintaining this park. We want to maintain a good relationship with the city and hopefully have lots more games like this in future years."

The Friends of Rickwood, helmed by the intrepid Gerald Watkins, is worthy of your donations. The nonprofit knows that the ballpark is a treasure entrusted by one father's generation to the next, and to the next.

And it needs to be protected so it will be enjoyed by generations to come. They will need to be reminded of how Rickwood Field reflects the turbulent, but ultimately triumphant, history of this vital Southern city.

And how, in the shadows of Birmingham's steel mills, it forged baseball's most iconic legends.

INDEX

A

Aaron, Henry 108, 110, 123, 134, 140
Abernathy, Woody 78
Adams Jr., Oscar W. 166
Adams Sr., Oscar W. 166
Alexander, Grover Cleveland 43, 44
Almeida, Rafael 111

B

Baldwin, Brooks 141
Bancroft, Billy 79, 80
Bando, Sal 120
Banks, Ernie 108
Barnes, Todd 151-153
Barr, Hyder 42
Bassett, Lloyd "Pepper" 89
Batiste, Jon 161
Belcher, Albert 111, 119
Belinsky, Bo 121
Bell, "Cool Papa" 20, 99
Bell, Gabby 118
Bender, Chief 77
Bernsen, Dutch 52, 53, 87
Bigelow, Elliot 65-68, 73, 101
Bloom, Curt 129, 137-139, 141-143
Blue, Vida 123
Bolton, Clyde 116, 118
Bonds, Barry 158, 162

Boseman, Chadwick 134
Boutwell, Albert 120
Breitenstein, Theodore 41
Brewer, David 13
Brown, April 144
Brown, Curly 47
Bruce, Bob 108
Bucknor, C.B. 160
Buffett, Jimmy 133
Burt, Jim 86, 129

C

Caldwell, Ray 14,74, 76-82, 116
Cameron, Mike 138, 139, 144
Campanella, Roy 110
Campaneris, Bert 120
Carson, Johnny 121
Cather, Bill 131
Charleston, Oscar 58, 99
Clarkson, Art 125-129
Clemens, Roger 133
Cobb, Ty 96-98, 126, 131, 133, 134
Cole, Jonathan O'Neil 57
Conigliaro, Tony 65
Connor, Bull 109, 110, 117, 118, 123
Cook, Murray150, 151
Costner, Kevin 131
Coveleski, Harry 36, 37, 39, 41, 42
Crosby, Tom 131
Crowder, "General" Alvin 74

D

Darnell, Henry 109
Davis, Joe 162
Davis, Piper 20, 78, 87, 88, 99 102-105, 164

Davis, Saul 59
Dean, Dizzy 14, 75, 76, 78-82, 121, 164
DeMoss, Bingo 63
Dempsey, Jack 115
DiMaggio, Joe 19, 20, 85
Dobbs, Johnny 66, 67, 74
Doby, Larry 104
Donahue, Mike 115
Donovan, Brendan 163
Dooin, Charlie "Red" 43, 44
Dreyfuss, Barney 52, 53
Dropo, Walt 18, 92, 101, 164
Duggleby, Bill 39
Duncan, Dave 120, 122, 159

E

Elko, Tim 141
Ellam, Roy 39
Emory, Lou 39
Escalante, Caylor 161

F

Farr, Alan 131
Feller, Bob 140
Fingers, Rollie 102, 120, 122, 159
Finley, Charlie 119, 121-123
Flynn, Jake 160
Folsom Jr., Jim 132
Ford, Harrison 134
Ford, Jason Michael 33
Forney, John 125
Foster, Andrew "Rube" 55, 57, 58, 64
Frazee, Harry 65

G

Gangl, Matt 162
Garagiola, Joe 17, 18
Gehrig, Lou 96
Gibson, Josh 20, 58, 88, 99, 134
Giles, Warren 90
Glazner, Whitey 52
Glennon, Eddie 91-95, 99, 101, 107, 111, 112, 114, 120
Gooden, Dwight "Doc" 133
Goodwin, Doris Kearns 20
Gordon, Alison 21
Gowdy, Curt 19
Grady, Henry 23, 24
Greason, Bill 110, 162
Greene, Justin 141
Greenwald, Doug 142, 143
Grich, Bobby 130
Griffey Jr., Ken 162
Grimes, Burleigh 47-49, 97
Grove, Lefty 62
Grzenda, "Shakey Joe" 108

H

Hall, Donald 17, 164
Handy, W.C. 89
Hardekopf, Bill 137, 138
Hardgrove, Omer 47
Hasty, Bob 74, 76, 81
Hayes, Walker 155
Heinkel, Don 127
Hemphill, Paul 117, 118
Henderson, Rickey 140
Hill, Benjamin 139-141
Hill, Carmen "Specs" 52

Hornsby, Rogers 97, 98

I

Iriarte, Jairo 141

J

Jackson, Reggie 102, 119-122, 140, 158, 159
Jackson, "Shoeless Joe" 41, 42
Jebeles, G.J. "Gus" 90, 91
Jeter, Derek 158
Johnson, Adrian 160
Johnson, Arthur 119
Johnson, Howard 127
Johnson, Walter 76, 79
Johnston, Jimmy 46, 47
Jones, Bobby 115
Jones, Tommy Lee 133
Jones, Ruben 60

K

Kaat, Jim 143
Kendrick, Bob 57, 159, 160
Killebrew, Harmon 139-141
Kiner, Ralph 99
Koplitz, Howie 108
Kronheim, David 144
Kurbin, Emily 160

L

Leavitt Jr., Charles W. 35
Lindo, Delroy 134
Lockett, Lester 88, 103
Longinotti, Frank 91
Ludolph, Willie 74

M

Mack, Connie 32-34, 71, 91-93, 100, 118, 126, 129, 133, 135
Manfred, Rob 165
Mantle, Mickey 96
Maranville, Rabbit 53
Marcan, Lil 42
Markham, John 89
Marmol, Oliver 159, 165
Marsans, Armando 111
Martin, Wayne 118
Marshall, Benny 115-118
Mathews, Eddie 135, 136
Mathewson, Christy 36, 43, 44, 97, 121
Matthews, Coke 131, 132, 136
Mays, Michael 162
Mays, Willie 20, 21, 96, 103-106, 127, 134, 140, 142-144, 154-156, 162, 164
Mays Sr., Willie 20, 21
McCurdy, Bill 81
McDowell, Jack 128, 129
McGilvray, Bill 41, 85
McGraw, John 36, 43, 97
McLain, Denny 126
McNamara, John 120, 121, 158, 159
McQueen, J. Williams 31
McWilliams, Jemel 161
Medwick, Joe "Ducky" 76, 78, 81
Mele, Al 87
Messenger, Bobby 36
Meusel, Emil "Irish" 51
Meyers, Lee 121, 122, 159
Milan, Clyde 74, 76, 79, 81
Mitchell, Chaz 148, 149, 165
Molesworth, Carleton 39, 45-47

Moore, Malachi 160
Moore, William J. 61, 62
Moran, Pat 44
Morgan, Jimmy 109
Morrison, Eugene 35
Morrison, "Jughandle Johnny" 52
Murray, Mitchell 61
Murphy, Dale 139
Musial, Stan 17-19, 99, 110, 166

N

Nelson, Jonathan 138, 139, 143-145
Newman, Zipp 75, 114, 115, 117, 118
Norton, Ed 83, 87

O

O'Brien, Tommy 101
O'Gara, Brian 153, 156, 157, 161, 162
O'Neil, Buck 134, 159, 160
Ordóñez, Magglio 139

P

Paige, Satchel 20, 59-64, 75, 88, 96, 103, 115, 121, 123, 134, 164
Pallante, Andre 163
Palmer, Jim 123
Palys, Stan 108
Paprocki, Jeremiah 160
Parsons, Charlie 24
Peel, Homer 81
Perdue, Frank M. 58
Petitti, Tony 147
Phillips, Bob 118
Piersall, Jimmy 65, 108
Pollard, Sam 134
Porter, Alan 160

Pratt, Derrill "Del" 39

Q

Quero, Edgar 141

R

Radcliffe, Ted "Double Duty" 88
Ramos, Heliot 163
Reagan, Ronald 118
Regan, Phil 108
Ritter, Lawrence 14
Robbins, Tim 131
Robinson, Brooks 123
Robinson, Jackie 99, 104, 110, 134
Rodriguez, Alex 158
Rollins, Rondal 127
Rose Jr., Pete 139
Rudi, Joe 102, 120, 122, 159
Rudi, Sharon 159
Ruth, Babe 65, 87, 96, 98, 115, 126, 134

S

Sabathia, C.C. 144
Salmon, Harry "Fish" 59, 60
Scruggs, Josiah Hubert 35
Seilor, Harold 93
Shelton, Ron 130-136
Sherrill, Dr. John 93
Shibe, Ben 32
Slaughter, Terry 131, 132
Sloss, Colonel Jacob 28
Smoltz, John 162
Southworth, Billy 51
Spahn, Warren 19
Speaker, Tris 41, 77

Stearnes, Norman "Turkey" 58
Stewart, Stuffy 73, 85
Stone, Naylor 118
Strawberry, Darryl 139
Streeter, "Spitballing Sam" 59, 60
Studdard, Ruben 158
Stump, Al 133, 134
Styles, Chuck 157
Suttles, George "Mule" 56, 59, 103

T

Taylor, Ben 58
Taylor, Charles Isam 55-58
Taylor, Zach 79, 80
Tenace, Gene 123
Thomson, Bobby 96
Tilden, Bill 115
Traynor, Pie 53, 54, 164

U

Underwood, Blair 134

V

Van Doren, Mamie 121, 122
Van Hoose, Alf 100, 116-118
Vecsey, George 113

W

Wagner, Honus 48, 49, 96, 97
Walkup, "Little Jimmy" 74, 76
Watkins, Gerald 147-149, 167
Weaver, Earl 123
Weis, Art "Butch" 73
Wells, Eddie 73
Wilkinson, J.L. 57, 58

Williams, Bulldog 50
Williams, Ted 19, 99
Williamson, Mykelti 134
Wilson, Artie 87, 102, 104, 105
Wilson, George 18, 101
Wilson, Glenn 127
Winn, Masyn 159
Wolfe, Thomas 22
Wood, Smoky Joe 65
Woodfin, Randall 157
Woodward, Bob 166, 167
Woodward, Joseph Hersey 22, 28-31, 39, 40, 50, 51, 85, 166
Woodward II, Joseph Hersey 85
Woodward, Rick 22, 29-31, 33-39, 43-48, 50-54, 56, 66, 68, 69, 71, 74, 80, 83-86, 91, 92, 97, 100, 101, 111, 114, 115, 118, 119, 129, 133, 164, 166
Woodward Jr., Rick 166
Woodward III, Rick 166
Woodward, Stimpson Hersey 28
Woodward, William H. 28

Y

Yaryan, Clarence Everett "Yam" 73
Yolkut, Jeremiah 153

Z

Zauchin, Norm 94, 101, 107

ABOUT THE AUTHORS

Tim Whitt is the author of *Bases Loaded With History* which told the story of Rickwood Field through the twentieth century. He first discovered Rickwood as a graduate student in Birmingham in the 1980s, and his interest in the history of the old Southern Association was further piqued working on a documentary about the league in the 1990s. For the last quarter of a century, he has been under contract to Michelle and has no intention of becoming a free agent. An Alabama native, he lives in Montgomery.

Name a ballpark, and **Joe Mock** has likely visited and scrutinized it, generating content for his BaseballParks.com site. In his role as sports-facilities beat writer for USA TODAY, he's written over 125 articles, including on-site reporting on MLB's three-day event at Rickwood Field in 2024. He's attended games at every MLB, spring training and affiliated Minor League venue, making him a ballpark afficionado of the highest order. He lives with his wife and dog in a suburb of Austin.

www.ingramcontent.com/pod-product-compliance
Lightning Source LLC
LaVergne TN
LVHW021655030226
830918LV00006B/21
* 9 7 8 1 9 6 5 7 6 6 5 2 1 *